Internet Guide
for
Rehabilitation
Professionals

Internet Guide
for
Rehabilitation
Professionals

Kathlyn L. Reed, PhD, OTR, FAOTA
Adjunct Professor
School of Occupational Therapy
Texas Woman's University
Houston, Texas

Sandra Cunningham, PhD, LOTA, FAOTA
Associate Professor of Occupational Therapy
School of Allied Health Professions
Louisiana State University Medical Center
New Orleans, Louisiana

Lippincott
Philadelphia • New York

Assistant Editor: Patricia L. Moore
Project Editor: Gretchen Metzger
Production Manager: Helen Ewan
Production Coordinator: Kathryn Rule
Design Coordinator: Lisa Caro
Indexer: Michael Ferreira

9 8 7 6 5 4 3 2 1

Library of Congress Cataloging in Publications Data

Reed, Kathlyn L.
    Internet guide for rehabilitation professionals/Kathlyn L. Reed,
Sandra Cunningham.
        p.   cm.
    Includes index.
    ISBN 0-397-55463-X (alk. paper)
    1. Medical rehabilitation—Computer network resources.
2. Communication in rehabilitation.   I. Cunningham, Sandra.
II. Title.
RM950.R43   1997
004.67'8'024617—dc21   97-4181
                                                                CIP

Care has been taken to confirm the accuracy of the information presented and to describe generally accepted practices. However, the authors, editors, and publisher are not responsible for errors or omissions or for any consequences from application of the information in this book and make no warranty, express or implied, with respect to the contents of the publication.

The authors, editors, and publisher have exerted every effort to ensure that drug selection and dosage set forth in this text are in accordance with current recommendations and practice at the time of publication. However, in view of ongoing research, changes in government regulations, and the constant flow of information relating to drug therapy and drug reactions, the reader is urged to check the package insert for each drug for any change in indications and dosage and for added warnings and precautions. This is particularly important when the recommended agent is a new or infrequently employed drug.

Some drugs and medical devices presented in this publication have Food and Drug Administration (FDA) clearance for limited use in restricted research settings. It is the responsibility of the health care provider to ascertain the FDA status of each drug or device planned for use in their clinical practice.

To those who have led the way onto the
Internet for rehabilitation personnel

Contents

UNIT I

INTRODUCTION TO THE INTERNET

CHAPTER 1

■■■■■■■■■■■■■■■■■■■■■■■■■■■■■■■■

Getting Started

The Internet is one of the fastest growing forms of communication today. As part of the Information Superhighway it will be shaping the way people think about communication and entertainment for the foreseeable future. Like many popular new ideas, soon people will wonder what life was like before the Internet became part of their lives. Although currently, using the Internet requires special equipment, in the near future access may be as easy as changing the television remote to another channel.

WHAT THE INTERNET IS

At its most basic form the Internet is an INTER-connected NETwork of networked computers. That is, computers linked together locally can also be linked together all over the world (Fig. 1-1). No central computer controls the worldwide network of computers. Instead the Internet relies on participation with each network performing its function in the whole. There are accepted "rules of the road" or protocol regarding software. The Internet uses transmission control protocol/Internet protocol (TCP/IP) as its standard. This protocol divides a message or file into small packets of electronic code that are all addressed to the receiving host computer and person connected to that host computer. When the packets arrive they are put back in order to form the original message or file. The Internet also has built-in redundancy so that when a packet cannot be routed one way, it can be redirected another way, as illustrated in Figure 1-2. All host computers must have electronic addresses so the correct packets can be sent to them. These addresses must be unique. If two addresses were

FIGURE 1-1. Internet access is worldwide.

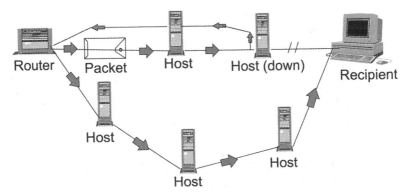

FIGURE 1-2. If a packet cannot proceed along one path it can be routed to another.

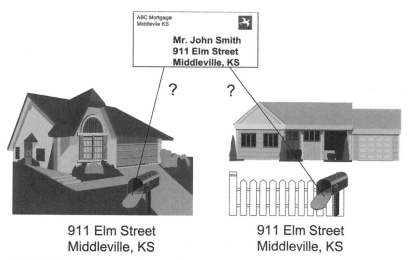

FIGURE 1-3. Just as two house addresses cannot be the same, two host computer addresses cannot be the same.

the same there would be confusion just as would occur if two houses had the same address (Fig. 1-3).

HOW THE INTERNET WORKS

Although the Internet is worldwide, the largest number of users are in the United States. The worldwide network is maintained by a variety of dedicated telephone lines, satellites, microwaves, and other devices (Fig. 1-4). The Internet in the United States is maintained primarily over large telephone lines. The three large switching stations, called network access points (NAPs), are located at San Francisco, Chicago, and New York. The headquarters for the metropolitan area ethernets, known also as metropolitan area exchanges (MAEs), is in Washington, DC and is often considered the fourth NAP. The three NAPs plus seven MAEs, plus two old military links known as Fix-East (Federal Internet Exchange) and Fix-West and one old commercial link called CIX (Commercial Internet Exchange) form the major access points or first level of access to the Internet in the United States. The 13 peer-interconnected points and their locations are shown in Figure 1-5. Nationally the switching stations are connected by nine large systems of lines (Fig. 1-6) that form the second level of access. Two of the biggest are InternetMCI (Washington, DC) and Sprint IP Services (Kansas City, MO). The others are PSINet (Performance System International), BBN Planet/AT&T WorldNet (Bolt, Beranek and Newman Planet), MRS Communications/UUNET Technologies, CRL Network Services, AGIS (Apex Global

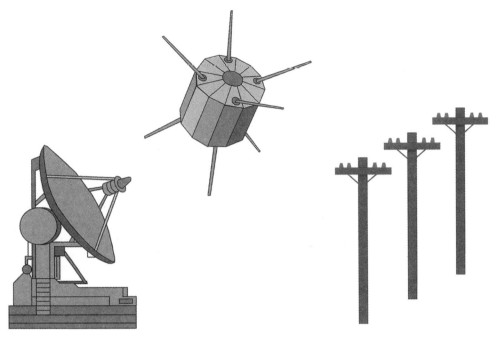

FIGURE 1-4. Internet makes use of telephone lines, satellites, and microwaves for connections.

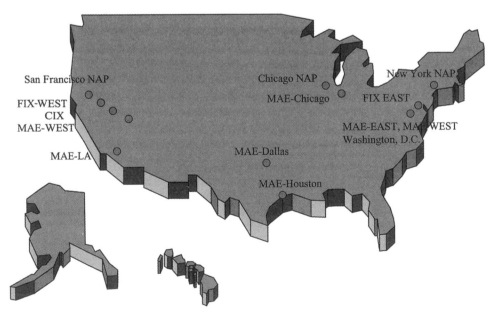

FIGURE 1-5. Major access points to the Internet in the United States.

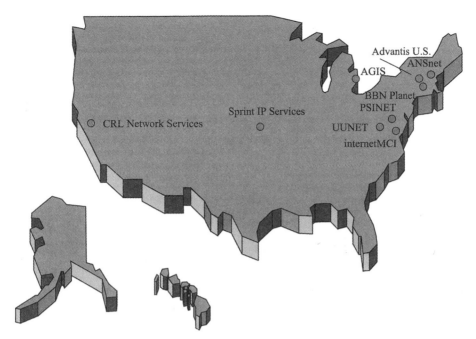

FIGURE 1-6. National backbone operators.

Information Services), ANSnet/AOL/GNN (Advanced Network and Services/American Online Line/Global Network Navigator), and IBM Global Network. Regional networks are located in many states, which link together to form the third level. Generally high-speed lines connect major cities; access to small cities and rural areas is through dedicated lines or modems. Internet Service Providers form the fourth level of access and the consumer and business market form the fifth level.

COUNTING NUMBERS

No one knows for sure how many people are linked together by the Internet. Most numbers are guesses because no one has actually counted. In January 1996, the number of host computers registered was 9,472,000 (Rickard, 1996a).

By summer the estimated number had increased to 16,999,348 (Rickard, 1996b). Since 1991 the number of host computers has nearly doubled each year (Fig. 1-7). Whether the trend can continue is not clear, but the Internet is obviously very popular. The numbers can be checked at http://www.nw.com.

The best estimate of the number of users is based on a survey done by O'Reilly & Associates in which about 200,000 telephone numbers were surveyed

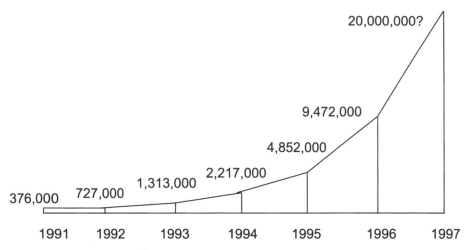

FIGURE 1-7. Doubling of the number of host computers each year.

to find out if people had access. Based on these estimates, about 13 million people have Internet access. On the other hand, a study at Vanderbilt University places the number at 28.8 million ("How Many People," 1996). The estimate is that about 4% of Americans use the Internet (Rickard, 1996b).

Of the host addresses, over 60% are in the United States. This percentage should drop as more people in other countries gain access. North America, Australia, and Europe have good access to the Internet. Africa is the most unrepresented continent (Rickard, 1996a); only South Africa has any noticeable presence on the Internet. The five countries with the highest Internet access are the United States, Germany, United Kingdom, Australia, and Japan. The countries with significant numbers of registered hosts are listed in Display 1-1. According to the NRIPE Network Coordination Centre, 239 countries have Internet codes. The list is available at gopher://ns.ripe.net/00/iso/codes.

Based on host computer addresses, the largest groups of users are in the domains of education (edu) and commercial (com). In contrast, international (int) organizations have the fewest addresses, followed by network organizations (net), government (gov), non-profit organizations (org), and military (mil).

In the Vanderbilt study, 16% of users defined themselves as "hard-core Web users" who had used the Web frequently in the past 24 hours. Twenty-one percent said they were "regular" users who had accessed the Web several times in the past week. Thirty-seven percent said they were "occasional" users who had used the Web within the past several months; 26% said they were "infrequent users." On the Internet as a whole most people classified themselves as "regular" users. The study also found that 73% of Web users are men and 17% are women. On the Internet as a whole 66% are men and 34% are women ("How Many People," 1996).

DISPLAY 1-1. NUMBERS OF HOST COMPUTERS IN COUNTRIES ON THE INTERNET

Countries with more than 55,000 host computers based on domains
United States
Germany
Canada
Australia
Japan
Finland
Netherlands
Sweden
France
Norway
Switzerland
Italy

Countries with 20,000–55,000 host computers based on domains
Spain
New Zealand
Austria
Denmark
South Africa
Belgium
Israel
Korea
Taiwan
Poland
Singapore
Brazil

Countries with 8,000–20,000 host computers based on two-letter domains
Hong Kong
Czech Republic
Russian Federation
Mexico
Hungary

Russia
Portugal
Chile
Greece
Iceland
Slovenia
Turkey
Argentina
Malaysia
Estonia
Thailand
Slovakia
Indonesia
Ukraine
Columbia
Croatia
China

Countries with 400–2,000 host computers
Philippines
Luxembourg
Lativia
Costa Rica
Kuwait
Venezuela
Bulgaria
Romania
Peru
India
Lithuania
Uruguay
Bermuda
Egypt
Faroe Islands
Ecuador

INTERNET COORDINATION

Although it is true there is no central control of the Internet, guidance and coordination do exist. Without some "rules of the road" the Internet would not function at all. From 1969 to 1992, guidance and coordination were provided by various agencies associated with the U.S. government through research and development projects sponsored by Advanced Projects Research Agency (APRA), National Science Foundation (NSF), National Aeronautical and Space Administration (NASA), and the Department of Energy (DOE). Much of the impetus for the funding was to gain military advantage during the Cold War period. When the Soviet Union collapsed, the military objective was no longer a priority and funding was discontinued.

Today the main guidance and coordination are provided by the Internet Society (ISOC), which was formed in 1992 as a private, nonprofit, international professional organization. Its purpose is to promote and facilitate Internet use through global cooperation and coordination. Formation was hastened by the concern that research funding from the United States government was being withdrawn and that no other source of coordination was readily available. The Internet had become too valuable as a medium of communication to let it disintegrate.

The ISOC is located in Reston, Virginia but has branch groups around the world. It can be reached at http://info.isoc.org. A frequently asked questions (FAQ) file is available at http://info.isoc.org/whatis/what-is-isoc.html. The ISOC operates with a Board of Trustees composed of 18 individuals selected worldwide. Individual and organizational memberships are available. To become an individual member, point a web browser to http:info.isoc.org/membership/individual-joint.html and complete the membership form available online. Individual membership is $35 per year and student membership is $25. Commercial organizations pay $10,000. Each applicant indicates whether all E-mails and regular mailings are to be sent, only official mailings, or no mailing. The money is used to support the standards-making activities of the Internet through the auspices of the ISOC.

The ISOC supports the work of the Internet Engineering Task Force (IETF). The IETF is the group of network designers, operators, vendors, and researchers who are concerned about the evolution of the Internet architecture and the continuing operation of the Internet. The purpose is to provide engineering protocols and develop standards for use on the Internet. The work of the IETF is accomplished through working groups with names like Applications, Network Management, Routing Security, and others who report to meetings held three times a year. Although membership is open to anyone, the information discussed is, as the work group names suggest, quite technical. For "techies" this is the site that explains in detail how the Internet actually operates including full text of the documents that detail how the standards should work. The IETF can be reached at http://www.ietf.org.

After the standards are developed and tested they are considered by the Internet Engineering Steering Group (IESG) for adoption. The IESG is composed of the area directors of the IETF and the chairman of the IETF. If there is dissension regarding adoption of a standard, the appeal goes to the Internet Architecture Board (IAB).

The IAB is responsible for overall architectural considerations (structure) of the Internet and adjudicates disputes in the standards process (function). Among the architectural standards is the TCP/IP. The IAB has 13 members who serve 2-year terms. Membership is based on nomination from the IETF and is approved by the ISOC.

A fourth group is the Internet Research Task Force (IRTF), a subgroup of the IAB, which tackles the long-term issues that will affect the Internet and network technology in the coming years. One question the IRTF is tackling is how the Internet will function when there are a billion users or if 100,000 homes in the United States were all wired for the Internet via cable television, not telephones.

A fifth group is the Internet Assigned Numbers Authority (IANA), which is the central coordinator for the assignment of numbers used in Internet protocol addresses such as ports and sockets. The IANA is chartered by the ISOC and the Federal Network Council (FNC). The FNC is an organization that coordinates the networking standards of the United States government agencies.

Another important guidance and coordinating group is the InterNIC (Internet Network Information Center), formed by the NSF in 1993 as a 5-year project. The InterNIC is actually a consortium of three groups. General Atomics provides a reference desk called the Net Scout Services by scouring the Internet for useful information and tools that can help the user explore the Internet. The Support Services provides more detailed information for the educators and researchers. AT&T provides the Directory and Data Base Services, which gives information on a variety of data bases, search tools, standards documents, and special projects. Networking Solutions provides the Internet Registration Service, which assigns IP (Internet protocol) addresses and registers addresses (the numbers no one remembers) and the domain names (the letters everyone must remember) with the Domain Name System. Without assignment and registration, addresses might be duplicated and some people would not get their messages and some host computers would be bypassed. In addition addresses must be formatted differently for different Internet services. Figure 1-8 shows some of types of addresses found on the Internet. The InterNIC, which can be reached at http://internic.net, also

kittyr@library.tmc.edu

This a personal E-mail address. Note the @ (at) sign. Individual internet addresses always have the @ sign in them.

ils.library.tmc.edu

This is the address of a host computer. Each host computer also has a numeric address such as 192.68.30.100. The host computer address can be used to Telnet to a host computer.

ftp.cs.orst.edu
This is an internet address for a FTP server.

http://www.library.tmc.edu
This is a World Wide Web address. Web addresses always include a colon and two forward slashes (://).

FIGURE 1-8. Understanding the different types of Internet addresses.

provides complete information for registering an IP and domain name address if the individual wants to create a site on the Web. Through the Whois, all sites with IP addresses and domain names on the Internet can be tracked.

Finally, there is the World Wide Web Consortium (W3C), which created and maintains the Web. The group is supported and funded by numerous large companies including Microsoft, Novell, NCSA (National Center for Supercomputing Applications), MCI, and AT&T. The W3C Web is a major resource for information about the Web including a subject directory of topics on the Web and a major reference for software and ideas to build a Web site. The Technical Areas provide computer language specification, graphics formats, fonts, protocols, and much more for the "do it yourself" Web page builder. The W3C can be reached at http://www.w3.org.

REFERENCES

How many people are there in cyberspace? (1996). *Internet Medicine: A Critical Guide, 1*(5), 7.
Rickard, J. (1996a). Internet numbers redux. *Boardwatch Magazine, 10*(4), 86–87.
Rickard, J. (1996, Summer). Introduction to the Boardwatch directory of Internet service providers. *Internet Service Providers: Boardwatch Special,* pp. 4–5.

CHAPTER 2

■■■■■■■■■■■■■■■■■■■■■■■■■■■■■■■■■■■■■

What's on the Net?

The Internet provides access to a variety of different types of services. Some services are possible only through the Internet, whereas others do not require the Internet to function but can make use of the Internet. The general categories are:

E-mail (electronic mail)
Mailing lists (Listservs)
Bulletin Board System (BBS)
Netgroups (called Usenets)
Archie or ArchiePlex
File transfer (FTP)
Telnet (Telephone net)
Online services
Internet relay chat (IRC)
Gopher
Wide Area Information Server (WAIS)
World Wide Web (WWW, Web)

The primary services on the Internet are E-mail, file transfer, and Telnet. The other Internet services grew from the basic services except bulletin board services and news groups, which were telephone services and do not require transmission control protocol/Internet protocol (TCP/IP) to run. Figure 2-1 shows the progression from primary or traditional Internet applications to the secondary or later generation applications.

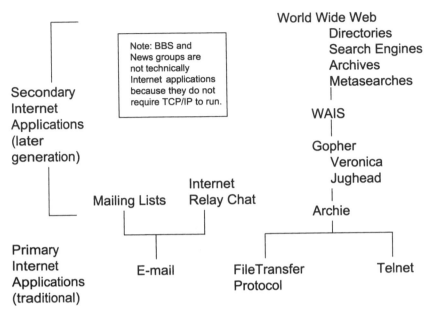

FIGURE 2-1. Overview of Internet services.

E-MAIL

E-mail is the most popular and widely known Internet service. E-mail, electronic letters and memos, can be sent and received any time of day and any day of the week. It can be sent and received over long distances in a short period of time. For example, a message from Australia might take less than 10 minutes to be received in Houston, Texas. The exact time depends on the total amount of traffic on the Internet and host computers. Although the telephone is faster, both parties must have access to a telephone at the same time. E-mail does not require that both parties be present at the same time although many E-mail systems will alert the user when new messages are received. Now there is even less excuse for "not writing."

MAILING LISTS

Mailing lists take advantage of the E-mail system. The difference is that each person on the mailing list receives the same message. Figure 2-2 shows a sample of how mailing lists work. Mailing lists allow people with similar interests to communicate with each other without having to send a separate E-mail to each person. Everybody on the mailing list gets the same E-mail so everyone gets the same information. It follows that only one message needs to be sent to the cen-

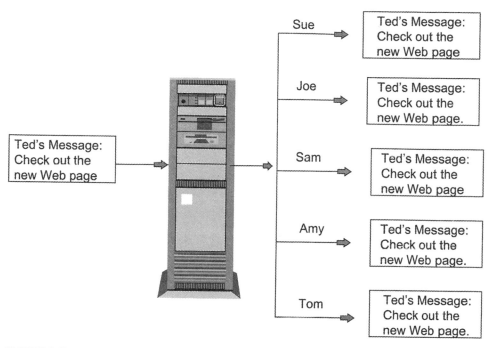

FIGURE 2-2. A mailing list sends a copy of a message to everyone on the list.

tral host computer because the host computer will distribute the message to everyone on the mailing list.

Most mailing lists are moderated, that is, a person is officially in charge of maintaining the mailing list. Tasks included making sure the host computer program is functioning correctly; adding and subtracting names as people join or leave the list; and reminding the members to stay on the subject, use good electronic manners, and keep people off the list who do not qualify for list membership.

Mailing lists cover a wide range of topics and new ones are added every day. Selecting mailing lists to join should be done carefully. The volume of incoming E-mail can quickly become overwhelming and use time needed for other tasks. Joining the Internet world does not necessarily save time.

BULLETIN BOARD SYSTEM

Electronic bulletin board systems called BBSs have been popular for many years. A BBS requires some disk space on a computer and a telephone number to contact the computer. Originally, most BBSs were reached through telephone lines and modems (Fig. 2-3) although people with mainframe computers could use IP addresses. Many BBSs still remain in this venue. Some BBSs now are also accessible through the Internet using a Telnet or remote log in connection. To view a BBS one dials the modem number for the BBS and selects from a menu those items one wishes to view. The information on the BBS is determined and controlled by the bulletin board system operator (sys op). The sys op is the only person who can change the information although some sys ops provide space for users to make suggestions and comments.

Electronic BBSs, like mailing lists, are available on many different subjects. The main differences between mailing lists and electronic bulletin boards are that mailing lists are more interactive and allow exchange of different viewpoints in a dynamic interchange. One reads a BBS; there is no membership list. BBSs are more static. One cannot interact directly with other readers although some BBSs allow readers to leave messages for other readers. Of course, the addressed reader must dial onto the bulletin board to get the message. It does not come automatically to one's computer. BBSs are more effective for providing detailed information that can be reviewed over a long period of time. Detailed information on a mailing list needs to be sent periodically because new members may not have received the previous mailing. Both BBSs and mailing list connects can be archived or organized into a series of frequently asked questions (FAQs), thus making them similar.

FIGURE 2-3. Electronic bulletin boards are similar to bulletin boards in a hallway at work or in a public building.

FIGURE 2-4. News groups include such subjects as card playing, pets, sports, cars, wine drinking, cooking, books, and travel.

NEWS GROUPS

News groups are the third variety of communication between people using telephones, modems, and computer disk space. Like mailing lists and BBSs, news groups are established around certain subjects or interests (Fig. 2-4). Unlike mailing lists and BBSs, news groups are not usually moderated. The users must moderate themselves, which sometimes works well and sometimes not. Anyone can submit a message to any news group because there is no membership requirement. Questions may be submitted and never be answered. The originator of the question can always try again. On the other hand, there is no moderator to stop a topic if users repeat the same theme again and again. In other words, news groups belong to the buyer beware mentality. News groups can be dynamic, entertaining, and informative, but they can also be boring and insulting.

Many news group messages are either in digest or archive form. The digest form summarizes the major points but does not usually save all the messages in their original form. Archiving stores the messages. News group messages may be archived by the thread (theme, subject, or topic) or by the date. Some search systems such as Dejanews specialize in archiving news group messages.

ARCHIE

Archie, one of the earliest programs developed on the Internet, was designed to help people negotiate the Internet. Originally a person had to remember or keep individual notes about the location of interesting or needed files on various computer directories. As the number of computers on the Internet increased, the human memory system and notation systems became stretched to the limit. New users were at a real disadvantage unless they had a good friend or mentor who would share information. Enter Archie. Archie is a computer program that visits other computers and copies their directory files for storage on a specific computer.

Actually there are several Archie computers around the world. A person who wants to know what is available in various directories connects to an Archie server and types in a request. The Archie server searches its data base of computer directory files that match the request and reports back the results. Now the user knows which computers have the information the user wants or needs. The user then connects to a selected computer directly, locates the files of interest, and views them. Archie programs work well but are labor intensive. A knowledge of Unix commands is also necessary because most mainframe computers use the Unix computer language to communicate. Learning the language is another barrier to use of the Internet.

FILE TRANSFER PROTOCOL (FTP)

Locating and viewing files of interest is usually the first step people do on the Internet, but often a user wants to copy a specific file to his or her own computer. Facilitating that process is the function of a file transfer program. The FTP client was developed to permit a user to download computer files from one computer to another. The user connects to another computer using the FTP client and locates a file on that computer to be downloaded. Commands are issued that instruct the two computers to link together for the purpose of transferring the file. Once the file is transferred the linkage is discontinued. The loaded file is then uploaded onto the receiving computer and made available for use.

Transferring files is an effective method of providing access to many different types of computer files. The process also facilitates the transfer of virus programs, which can destroy data files and cause the computer to malfunction. Whenever a file is downloaded, it should always be scanned for viruses before being uploaded. "Safe computing" can save time, energy, and equipment.

TELNET

Telnet or telephone network is a protocol that facilitates remote log on to another computer. Remote log on is useful for exploring large data bases such as library catalogs. The remote log on protocol permits the user to manipulate the data base as if the user were accessing the data base from a terminal at the location as the data base computer. Most often the user can read the data base but cannot write to or change the data base. The user may be able to write short messages to the data base operator. Many library catalogs are still accessible via Telnet.

Remote log on is not limited to data bases. Many universities also use Telnet connections to permit students to register for classes offsite. Forms required for registration are available on the menu. The student selects the necessary form, completes it, and signs off. The registrar retrieves the form and completes the registration process.

ONLINE SERVICES

Many online services such as America Online, CompuServe, Prodigy, Delphi, and others make use of Telnet connections to provide users with an array of services, some of which are interactive. Services may include access to encyclopedias, dictionaries, cook books, airline schedules, travel planners, electronic mail, bulletin board, special interest groups, Internet relay chat, information on buying and using computers, computer shopping, computer software, computer help groups, world and national news, weather, sports, financial planning, stock quotes, household budgeting, medical data bases, health information, entertainment news, games, movie reviews, music groups, educational opportunities, lists of colleges and universities, census information, job listings, Internet access, and much more (Fig. 2-5). Online services are multipurpose computer access systems. Of course, such a smorgasbord of services is not free. Online services charge a monthly fee, typically $20 per month for unlimited connect time. For premium services such as access to searching MEDLINE, there may be additional fees because the MEDLINE system charges the online service.

Online services are extremely popular. America Online and CompuServe are the largest. Whether a person gets his or her money's worth depends on whether all the services are of value to the individual or family. Most of the services listed are now available over the Internet. Internet services are becoming cheaper.

FIGURE 2-5. Games, magic, and more are available through online services.

Depending on which services are of value and how much time is spent, Internet services may be cheaper and offer even wider access.

INTERNET RELAY CHAT

Internet relay chat (IRC) is a real-time, multiuser client program that allows the user to "talk" with other Internet users interactively using the keyboard as a communication tool. There are dozens of "channels" on a wide variety of subjects for young and old, male and female, conservative and liberal, athletes and couch potatoes, indoor and outdoor, plus numerous other groups. There are no national boundaries on the Internet. IRC groups can include people from all over the "global village." Real names are not used. Instead everyone is identified by a nickname. IRCs can provide useful information or waste spare time. Choose the channels carefully.

GOPHER

Gopher is an Internet protocol that organizes computer directories into a series of hierarchical menus, an improvement over the Archie protocol. A search on an Archie computer provides the source information but does not provide a computerized link to that source. The user still has to establish the link. Gopher is a big improvement over Archie in that regard. The protocol that searches computers using Gopher is called Veronica. Computers using the Veronica search system are located through the world. After selecting a Veronica site, the user types in a search request and the Veronica program looks through its files for matching sites throughout the world. These sites are organized into a list with numbers attached. The user types in the number of the site or highlights the line and the computer makes a connection to the that site.

A modification of the Veronica program is called Jughead. The Jughead program looks through the files on a single computer rather than many computers. As mainframe computers increased in size and number of files, some computers became storehouses of information. The need arose for an organizer and indexer of the mountain of information on just one big computer. Jughead serves that purpose.

The Gopher protocol was the first program that made using the Internet feasible for most users. There is no need to know Unix commands and there is direct access to the document sources. Veronica and Jughead facilitated the search and location of files. Gopher is easy to use and understand. The user selects the number and types it on the computer. The users computer is automatically connected to that computer and the file is available for viewing, printing, or downloading.

The drawback to Gopher is it supports text or keyboard symbols only. Therefore photography graphics cannot be viewed on Gopher sites.

WIDE AREA INFORMATION SYSTEM (WAIS)

The WAIS sites were the next improvement after Gopher. The WAIS protocol permits every word to be searched, allowing the user to find information at a very detailed level. This format is ideal for some texts such as encyclopedias, the Bible, or the complete works of Shakespeare. The drawback is that WAIS-supported files use lots of computer memory and thus are relatively expensive to maintain. Also, they are primarily text files. A few WAIS sites still exist but most were overtaken by the emerging World Wide Web.

WORLD WIDE WEB

The Web is the latest and best advance in Internet protocol. The Web protocol is the most flexible format available. A Web page can include text in different-sized formats, graphic images, video clips, movie clips, sound clips, and music. Thus, the Web is truly a multimedia format. Web pages also can be linked to other pages by embedded links called hyperlinks or hotlinks. Any word on the page can become a hyperlink to another document on another computer or on the same computer. This linked arrangement is called associate language and is made possible by the programming language called hypertext markup language or HTML.

Web pages are increasing rapidly. Search systems have become necessary to find new sites of interest. Search engines are developing nearly as quickly as the Web pages themselves. Some of the best known are Lycos, AltaVista, Web-crawler, Inktomi, and Yahoo. Search engines are the indexes of the Internet. To look up a topic the user types the subject in the space provided and clicks on the search button. The search engine returns a list of sites that match the search request.

SUMMARY

The Internet offers something for everyone. The variety has grown large and is increasing. Access to the Internet is becoming easier and, in the next few years, may become as easy as turning on the television set. Worldwide information and entertainment are as close as the computer and monitor.

CHAPTER 3

■■■■■■■■■■■■■■■■■■■■■■■■■■■■■■■■■■■■■■

Equipment and Software Needs

Equipment and software needs depend on what is of interest on the Internet. Because the Internet provides a number of potential services, this chapter is divided into three sections: ideal, acceptable, and minimum. These suggestions are based on the assumption that access to the Internet is from home or from a small business such as a private clinic. A hospital or university will need larger and more expensive equipment than recommended in this chapter.

The pieces of equipment and software discussed include a computer, hard drive, monitor, modem, pointing device, operating system software, communications and Internet protocol software, Web browser, graphics card, sound card, speakers, CD-ROM, backup drive, and printer. Equipment is illustrated in Figure 3-1.

IDEAL EQUIPMENT

Ideal equipment is designed to take full access of the Internet features. The computer should have a fast central processing unit (CPU) running at over 100 megahertz (MHz) with 16 or more megabytes (MB) of dynamic memory and 1 gigabyte (GB) or larger hard drive; having two hard drives is even better. Graphic, video clips, and sound bytes can be very large files that require a lot of memory to load and even more memory to store. For an IBM or IBM clone computer a high-speed Pentium chip, the CPU, is preferable. For Apple Macintosh select a computer from the Performa or Power series. The color monitor should be 15 inches or larger with at least a 0.28 dot pitch screen that is super video graphics array (SVGA) compatible or better. If a modem is needed for a serial line Internet protocol (SLIP) or point-to-point protocol (PPP) account, the baud rate should be 28.8 (28,800) or better. For an integrated services digital network

Printer   Monitor

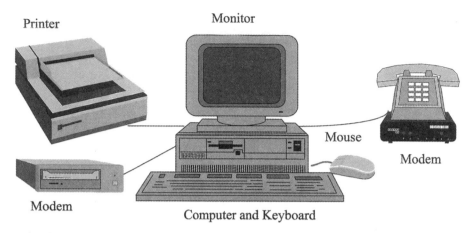

Mouse

Modem

Modem   Computer and Keyboard

FIGURE 3-1. Equipment needed to access the Internet.

(ISDN) connection a modem is not needed because the transmission signal remains digital but a transmission device is needed. The computer should have a mouse, trackball, trackpost, or glide. The operating system for IBM should be Windows 95, which can handle 32-bit applications or OS2, and for Apple Macintosh, System 7.5. The 32-bit access is needed to view files written in the JAVA programming language. Communication software is built into Windows 95 and is included in most Mac systems. Check to be sure that Internet access protocol, transmission control protocol/Internet protocol (TCP/IP), is available. Netscape Navigator 2.0 or higher is the recommended Web browser for both PC and Mac. A Telnet application for remote login is not available in Netscape but is available in Windows 95 or can be downloaded from the Internet. Netscape does provide a basic E-mail program but Eudora (shareware) or Eudora Plus 2.2 or higher (commercial) is recommended. WinZip is a good program for compressing and uncompressing files. The graphics card should be SVGA compatible or better and the sound card should be 16 bit or higher capable of full duplex. Mac sound cards are all full duplex but many PC sound cards are half duplex. The speakers should be the best affordable that can be attached to the sound card. Speakers built into or attached to a monitor or keyboard are generally small and have limited fidelity. Independent, free-standing speakers provide for a greater range of audio fidelity. The CD-ROM should be 6X or better with the capacity to write and read. Keeping and storing some large applications on CD-ROM is more efficient than keeping them on the hard drive. A backup tape drive is useful to provide copies of files in case of a system crash, which damages the hard drives, and for storing programs or files needed only occasionally. A color laser or ink jet printer is desirable for printing color files. The faster the printer can print a colored page, the better.

    All this equipment adds up to a princely sum and may require a king's ransom to purchase. Unless the bank account contains the winnings from the lottery or a Las Vegas jackpot, a carefully planned budget will be needed to acquire all

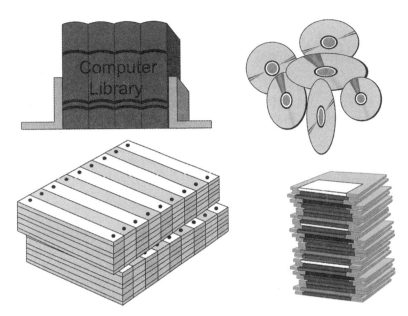

FIGURE 3-2. Other items needed are computer books, printer paper, CDs, and disks.

the ideal equipment. Space in an office or living quarters is also a consideration. This equipment will occupy the space on a full-sized desk. As Figure 3-2 shows, storage for floppy disks, CD-ROMs, computer books, software program manuals, and printer paper takes additional space. Think about the space needs before it becomes necessary to put the bed and sofa outside the front door.

ACCEPTABLE EQUIPMENT

Acceptable equipment provides access to most Internet features but does not provide all the bells and whistles of the ideal equipment. The computer may be of the 386 or 486 series for IBM and an SE that is color enabled or of the Performa series for Apple Macintosh running at 60 to 100 MHz. The dynamic RAM should be 8 to 12 MB with a hard drive storage capacity of 500 to 850 MB. The operating system can be Windows 3.1 or OS2 for IBM-type computers and System 7 or 7.5 for Macs. The monitor should be a 14-inch color, VGA with 0.51 dot pitch. The modem may be 14.4 baud (14,400). The TCP/IP protocol software will need to be installed. It is included (bundled) with most Web browsers and online services. The Web browser may be Netscape, Internet Explorer, Mosaic, Chameleon, Cello, or any other browser with graphics display potential (graphics enabled). A Telnet application is necessary. Other client programs such as E-mail, file transfer program (FTP), and Gopher are useful. A useful Web application to run movie and video clips is Quick Time. Audio files may require WAV, a format for storing sounds in files. A SVGA graphics card is required for the color monitor. The sound card, CD-ROM player, and backup storage drive are optional. A monochrome laser printer is useful for printing information located on the Internet.

MINIMAL EQUIPMENT

Minimal equipment and software provide access to a limited number of Internet features but do not allow access to useful features on the Internet. The computer may be a 286 or 386 series for IBM and an SE series for Apple Macintosh. Note that 8086, 8088 series of IBM-type computers and Apple II series computers are not recommended for Internet access although they can be used for some low-end functions such as E-mail and bulletin board activities. The CPU can be running at 16 to 50 MHz. The operating system may be DOS or Windows 2.0 for IBM and 5.0 for Macs. Be aware that an IBM computer must be at least a 386 to run Windows 3.1. Without a Windows operating system, the graphics on Web pages cannot be accessed. The monitor may be monochrome, which is fine for text files but does limit the visual quality of graphics. On-board dynamic memory may be 1 to 4 MB. Windows 3.1 requires 2 MB of dynamic RAM. The hard drive may be 40 to 450 MB. The modem may be 2,400 or 9,600 baud. Generally a 300 or 1,200 baud modem is not supported by most Internet hosts including the major online service providers such as American Online. Some do not support 2,400 baud. A communications program will be needed. Although many can be used, Pro-Comm (shareware), ProComm Plus (commercial), or ProComm for Windows is a good basic program. A video card is necessary to use the monitor and generally comes with the computer. A graphics card is needed for Windows software. A sound card and CD-ROM are not needed. A dot matrix printer is recommended for printing messages and text files. This equipment will allow access to E-mail, Listservs, chat groups, FTP, and Gopher sites. Web sites may be limited to text only using Lynx software. Lynx provides access to the text but does not support graphics. Downloading files from FTP sites may be extremely slow. Upgrading to better equipment and software is strongly encouraged as soon as the budget permits.

SUMMARY

Using and enjoying the Internet is an expensive hobby. If any of the expenses can be applied to a business, start keeping receipts with the tax records now. For birthday and Christmas gifts, suggest computer items. Keep a wish list attached to the monitor so everyone can see what is needed next. Most stores and mail order businesses allow a 30-day exchange period so if two items arrive, one can be returned for the next item on the list. Happy Interneting!

CHAPTER 4

■■■■■■■■■■■■■■■■■■■■■■■■■■■■■■■■■■■■

Access and Providers

ACCESS TO THE INTERNET

There are three types of connections to the Internet. The first is through a host computer known as a server that is connected to or part of a local area network (LAN) as shown in the upper right hand corner of Figure 4-1. A similar arrangement is shown in the upper left hand portion of Figure 4-1 except that the number of computers is greater and divided into parts jointed by a bridge computer and a router. The divided sets of computers form a wide area network (WAN). Both the LAN and WAN are examples of situations found in work environments such as hospitals, universities, or companies.

The majority of individuals connected to the Internet are currently using serial line Internet protocol (SLIP) or point-to-point protocol (PPP) connections. The SLIP and PIP connections require a modem to translate the digital signal of the computer to the analog signal of the telephone line, transporting the signal over the Internet and back to the digital form on the other end. Digital signals used in computers are composed of binary (meaning two) numerals. Analog signals are sine waves. Digital signals work in an off-on relationship, whereas analog signals work in a gradation from small to large. Figure 4-2 shows how the two forms differ using a standard light switch and a dimmer switch as examples.

Both SLIP and PPP connections still must go through a server or host computer to get to the Internet. The server or host is usually owned or leased to the Internet service provider (ISP). From the ISP, in turn, the user is connected to the Internet, although the connection may be through several routers not shown in Figure 4-1.

The third type of connection is through an integrated services digital network (ISDN), which is a digital circuit-switched network that can carry both voice and data communication over a single cable. An ISDN connection does not require a modem; there is no need to switch from digital to analog because the telephone

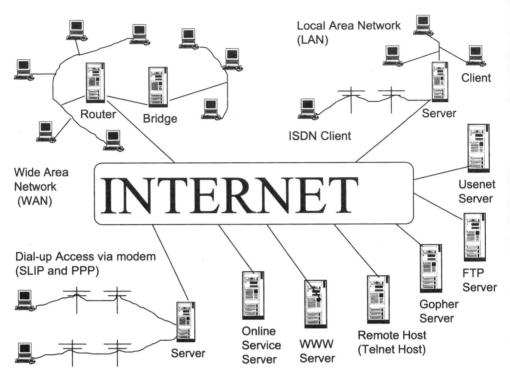

FIGURE 4-1. A simple model of the Internet.

lines are digital just as in the computer. These ISDN lines, however, are new and expensive where they are available. Not all locations have access to the ISDN lines. An example of an ISDN client is shown in the middle upper right portion of Figure 4-1.

The rest of Figure 4-1 shows some of the various servers to which a person with any one of the three types of connections to the Internet can access. The variety of services and servers on the Internet continues to grow.

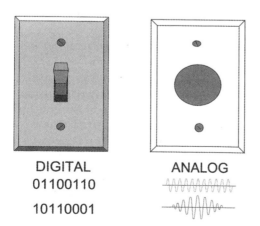

DIGITAL
01100110
10110001

ANALOG

FIGURE 4-2. Digital versus analog.

PROVIDERS AND GETTING CONNECTED

There are three major ways of connecting to the Internet. One way is through the work site as discussed above. Most computers at a work site are connected to a LAN. The LAN in turn is connected to the Internet. Some larger work sites may have several LANs that are joined together to form a WAN. The WAN is in turn connected to the Internet. The cost of the connection is paid by the company.

A second way is to join a major computer service such as America Online, CompuServe, or Prodigy. These services have Internet access as one of the options available from their selection menu. Most now provide Internet access to the most popular types of Internet tools. Computer services charge a monthly fee for their service, which is usually billed to a credit card number the user supplies when setting up the account. The typical cost for unlimited access to the Internet and other features of an online service is $19.95 per month.

The third way is dial-up access through an Internet service provider (ISP). There are three types of ISP accounts: SLIP, PPP, and ISDN. Both SLIP and PPP connections require a modem to translate the computer's digital signal to analog and back again. A SLIP connect is faster than a PPP connect, but the PPP is generally preferred over SLIP because PPP provides data compression and error correction, which means the signal is more likely to be correct. ISDN provides a direct connection. It not does require an analog modem because the telephone line is digital. ISDN is faster than SLIP or PPP. So what is the drawback? It is more expensive. SLIP or PPP accounts cost $20 to $40. ISDN accounts charge much more, depending on the ISP plan.

The ISPs can be divided into three divisions based on locale: national, regional, and local. There are advantages and disadvantages in selecting each. National and regional ISPs are generally easier to check out because they are widely known. Information about their strengths and weaknesses can be evaluated by asking about them on various review services online. Usually the advantages of national or regional ISPs are their knowledge of the Internet, their years in the Internet business, and the likelihood that they will remain in the Internet business. The disadvantage is that they often cannot provide much individual attention such as coming to your business or home to help with problems. Calls for help may be long distance without benefit of a toll-free number. Also there may be long distance charges for access to the Internet if there is no local code (telephone access) for that provider. The 10 largest ISPs are listed in Table 4-1.

Local providers can provide more individual services. They assess no long-distance charges if their area code is the same as the telephone line being used to access the Internet. The disadvantage of local providers is their small size; they may not survive in the business jungle and their knowledge of the Internet may be less extensive. Small providers also may have less capital to improve their equipment as new enhancements become available.

Because there is no best answer in selecting an ISP, the following are questions to think about and ask when selecting an ISP:

TABLE 4-1. LARGEST INTERNET SERVICE PROVIDERS			
Name	**Subscribers**	**Telephone Number**	**Home Page**
Netcom	435,000	408-983-5950	http://www.netcom/com
Spry Net*	145,000	206-957-8000	http://www.sprynet.com
Global Network Nav.†	145,000	703-918-1802	http://www.gnn.com
EarthLink	127,000	818-296-2400	http://www.earthlink.net
MindSpring	125,000	404-815-0082	http://www.mindspring.com
Concentric	115,000	517-895-0500	http://www.cris.com
IDT Corporation	114,800	517-928-1000	http://www.idt.net
Internet American	30,000	214-861-2999	http://www.airmail.net
TIAC	26,000	617-276-7200	http://www.tiac.net
CRL Network	11,000	415-837-5300	http://www.crl.net

*Subsidiary of CompuServe
†Subsidiary of America Online

1. What is the price structure for PPP or SLIP versus ISDN?
2. Is there a local access number in the city?
3. Is it possible to qualify for discounts?
4. Does the ISP offer software and hardware support? Is it a free call?
5. Which browser does the ISP support? Is the browser available from the ISP?
6. Does the ISP allow and support development of a homepage?
7. What Internet resources does the ISP provide and support?
8. Does the ISP provide security for credit card transactions?

CHAPTER 5

■■■■■■■■■■■■■■■■■■■■■■■■■■■■■■■■■■■■

A Brief History of the Internet

The development of the Internet began on January 2, 1969 with a Defense Department contract to explore how four university research computers, three in California and one in Utah, could be linked together. This linkage had to work even if the network experienced partial failure (eg, from a bombing). In military terms the logic was to create a linkage system that did not have a central computer through which all direction was given. If the linkage system could withstand partial failure, then an enemy could not totally destroy the communication network by knocking out the central computer. The project was called ARPANet (Advanced Research Projects Agency Network). The four universities were University of California at Los Angeles, University of California at Santa Barbara, Stanford Research Institute, and the University of Utah.

To solve the problem of bomb proofing the network, a program was created that divided each message into small packets with the address of the destination attached to all packets. When the packets were received the instructions also provided directions for reassembling the packets in the correct order. After several programs were tried the one selected as the standard was called transmission control protocol/Internet protocol (TCP/IP). TCP/IP is the communications protocol that makes the Internet work. In 1982, TCP/IP became a nonproprietary "suite" of protocols.

E-mail was developed in 1972 to deliver messages across the growing network of 40 host computers. The following year the network became international when England and Norway were connected. By 1977, the number of host computers had reached 100 (Fig. 5-1). In 1982, the Department of Defense created MILNET for military activities. Thus, there were two networks and the term Internet became accepted to describe the interconnection of two different networks.

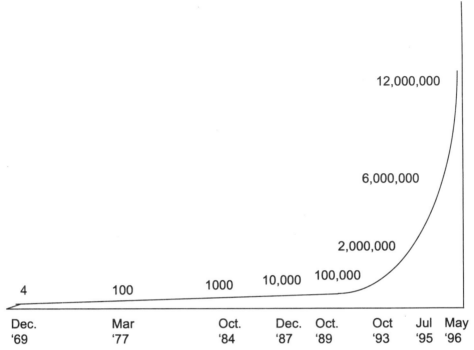

FIGURE 5-1. Number of host computers in the world.

By 1984, the number of host computers had increased to 1000, most of which were in universities or military installations. In the same year the domain name server (DNS) system was introduced, which permitted users to create letter combinations for Internet addresses instead of numbers, which were harder to remember in the right order. In 1986, the Department of Defense no longer wanted the responsibility of coordinating the Internet. The National Science Foundation (NSF) assumed responsibility for the Internet. NSFNet provided the Internet with a high-speed backbone operating at 56 Kbps (56,000 bits per second). The Cleveland FreeNet started operation in 1986 as the first Internet service.

By July 1988, the NSF network had increased the backbone of the Internet to 13 sites. Many of the 13 sites listed in Display 5-1 and shown in Figure 5-2 continue to be major contributors to the growing knowledge and use of the Internet. Their names appear frequently as major innovators and archival sites. The responsibility for keeping the backbone functioning was awarded to Merit Network, Inc. in partnership with IBM, MCI, and the State of Michigan. The partnership developed the Network Operations Center at Merit in Ann Arbor, Michigan. Merit functioned 24 hours a day.

In 1989, the number of hosts was 100,000 and the NSFNet backbone was upgraded to 1.544 Mbps (also called T1). That's 1.544 megabytes per second. Com-

DISPLAY 5-1. THE ORIGINAL 13 INTERNET SITES CREATED BY THE NATIONAL SCIENCE FOUNDATION

Merit—University of Michigan Computing Center at Ann Arbor, Michigan

BARRNet (Bay Area Regional Network) at Palo Alto, California

San Diego Supercomputer Center (University of California at San Diego) at San Diego, California

National Center for Atmospheric Research (NCAR) at Boulder, Colorado

SURANET (Georgia Tech) at Atlanta, Georgia

The National Center for Supercomputing Applications (NCSA) at the University of Illinois, Urbana-Champaign, Illinois

MIDnet (University of Nebraska) at Lincoln, Nebraska

Jon von Neumann Center (Princeton University) at Princeton, New Jersey

Cornell Theory Center (Cornell University) at Ithaca, New York

The Pittsburgh Supercomputing Center (University of Pittsburgh) at Pittsburgh, Pennsylvania

SESQUINET (Rice University) at Houston, Texas

Westnet (University of Utah) at Salt Lake City, Utah

NorthWestNet (University of Washington) at Seattle, Washington

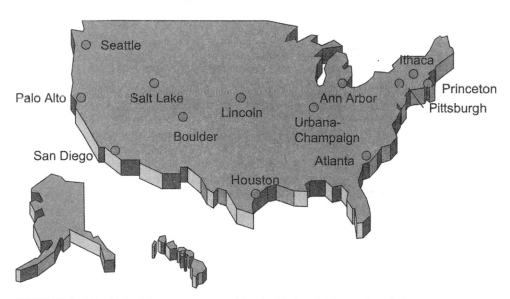

FIGURE 5-2. The 13 backbone sites created by the National Science Foundation.

puServe and MCI Mail set up Internet E-mail gateways. Commercial activities were first allowed on the Internet in 1991. Until 1991, the Internet was restricted to military, education, research, and nonprofit activities.

The World Wide Web was first announced in 1992 but did not become popular until the following year when Mosaic browser was released. That same year the backbone was increased to a T3 line (45 Mbps). The White House created a Web page in 1993 and permitted people to E-mail the President of the United States directly. The address is president@whitehouse.gov/.

Commercial advertising was first permitted in 1994 and is quickly making up for lost time. That same year digital video and audio transmission first occurred over the Internet.

The NSF bowed out of the Internet business in 1995 and the backbone lines were turned over to three network access points (NAPs) located at San Francisco (PacBell), Chicago (Bellcore and Ameritech), and New York (SprintLink). Security technologies became available to scramble signals so financial transactions could be carried out over the Internet. Enhanced compression technologies enabled multimedia programs to be sent via the Internet.

The Internet now functions with a mixture of government and private backbones. In addition to the three NAPs are two major Federal government Internet sites used to route MILNET, NASA Science Net, and other government messages. Originally the sites were restricted to military and government purposes only, but they now route nonmilitary messages as well. The two military sites are called FIX-EAST and FIX-WEST and are located at College Park, Maryland and Mountain View, California (Ames Research Center), respectively. In addition, a private commercial enterprise called the Commercial Internet Exchange (CIX) was started in 1991 to provide a commercial exchange for Internet traffic. CIX is located in Santa Clara, California.

Added to the six major Internet routing points are seven metropolitan area ethernet (MAEs) sites that were started by Metropolitan Fiber Systems, Inc. to provide large cities with a means of transmitting data quickly and efficiently using a fiberoptic ring. The fiberoptic concept adapted well to the growing structure of routers for the Internet and became part of the backbone structure. The seven MAEs are located in:

San Jose, California (MAE-WEST)
Los Angles, California (MAE-LA)
Dallas, Texas (MAE-DALLAS)
Houston, Texas, (MAE-HOUSTON)
Chicago, Illinois (MAE-CHICAGO)
Two in Washington, DC (MAE-EAST and MAE-WEST)

The Washington, DC sites are the hub of the MAEs. MAE-EAST is a superfast site operating at 100 Mbps. Anyone or any organization with a connection, direct or indirect, to an NAP, to a FIX, to CIX, or to an MAE has access to the Internet.

CHAPTER 6

■■■■■■■■■■■■■■■■■■■■■■■■■■■■■■■■■■■■■■■

Doing Rehabilitation on the Internet

Three groups are most likely to obtain information on rehabilitation from the Internet. First are consumers who want information on health concerns, second are those desiring to improve client care, and third are professionals who interact for various reasons.

CONSUMERS

The Internet offers opportunities for relating to consumers in ways that are familiar but different. Consumers have found the Internet to be a bonanza for creating support groups. The groups can include members from all over the world and members with disabling conditions that would have restricted their participation in local group meetings in the community. The Internet community is available anywhere a computer, modem, and telephone line can be situated. People confined to their homes can participate on the Internet. Traditional self-help or self-care groups have relied on some professional staff to keep the organization going. On the Internet anyone can organize and maintain a Listserv, newsgroup, or chat group. The system operator or system administrator may be a person with the disorder or disease for which the Listserv, newsgroup, or chat group was organized. The initiative of consumers on the Internet must be observed to be believed. Listservs and newsgroups cover all sorts of diseases and disorders that might have support groups in the larger cities. Examples include fibromyalgia, Lyme disease, and chronic fatigue syndrome. These groups share information and provide support over distances difficult to navigate without the Internet. They allow consumers and professionals to interact on a scale not possible until the Internet was formed.

As with any communications there are a few useful guidelines and frequently asked questions (FAQ). First, consumers do not like to be referred to as clients or patients. They are persons with a disorder, disease, or condition. (Note: the term disorder will be used for the remainder of this discussion for convenience.) Thus, the phrase is "a person with fibromyalgia" not "a fibromyalgia patient." If the person is a patient of the professional the preferred wording is "a person with fibromyalgia with whom I have worked or treated." People who have had the disorder for many years often refer to themselves as "survivors," but not as "long-term patients" or "clients." Second, consumers generally are open to having professionals participate in the group as long as the professionals do not preach "the gospel according to...." Professionals who believe there is only one way to approach or treat a disorder and insist on using cyberspace to make the point will get negative responses from consumers and may be cut off by the system operator. Third, the professional is likely to learn that persons with a specific disorder are asking many questions of each other but never asking a professional. An example is a person with epilepsy asking other consumers if anyone knows anyone who has died from an epileptic seizure. Professionals know the answer is no but do not seem to tell people with epilepsy that fact. Participation on a consumer group may cause the professional to rethink some of the information routinely provided to persons seen in rehabilitation. A number of questions may be addressed to relieve persons with specific disorders of much anxiety—anxiety and questions the professional did not realize existed.

So what role can the professional fulfill on a consumer-oriented help group? The professional can provide factual information and data and knowledge of techniques or approaches that are useful in managing life with the disorder. Facts include the known causes of the disorder, accepted diagnostic procedures, accepted procedures and treatment techniques, and known prognosis. Professionals can also emphasize that the cause of some disorders is unknown and that some procedures and treatment techniques are experimental or unproven. Other facts can be the names, addresses, and contact points (Internet address, telephone number, or fax number) for products and services useful to persons with a specific disorder. Professionals can state that local services may be as good as those many miles away to discount the notion that the "best" treatment is always at least 50 miles from home. Professionals can remind consumers to get a second or third opinion about controversial or conflicting diagnoses and treatments. Professionals can also cite books or journal articles that they know contain good factual information. However, the professional should consider the reading level of the information and warn consumers that professional literature may be difficult to understand unless the consumer has already learned many of the medical words pertaining to the disorder.

What should professionals not do over the Internet? The same rules apply to the Internet that would apply to attending a party or going out with a group of friends. One, do not diagnose or recommend treatment and resist the temptation to do so. Actually most consumers are aware of this fact and may intercede to recommend that the person see a local professional. Two, maintain confidentiality. Do not give information that is private about actual clients or patients, especially their names or addresses. Some Interneters may want to contact patients or clients the professional has seen. Do not be tempted to give out client or patient names without permission to do so. State that the contact will be made by you as a professional. If the patient or client wishes to make contact directly that is his or her prerogative.

Frequently asked questions include "What if a consumer starts talking about a wonderful cure that the professional knows is quackery, such as copper bracelets for treating arthritis?" Information about fake cures and outright quackery are generally known to experienced Interncters. One of them is likely to answer and the answer may carry more weight than that of a professional. It is important to remember that professionals are not necessarily regarded as the most knowledged people about the disorder. People who live with the disorder day in and day out feel they know much more about the disorder than professionals who can leave the disorder at the front door of the clinic or hospital.

What about posting standard information on the Internet such as warning signs for cancer, basic food groups, or possible side effects of drugs? Do not bother. Consumers on the Internet have a name for these prepared statements from professionals—shuttleware. Shuttleware is information that is simply transferred from one medium to another. The information is either not needed or ends up as part of the group's FAQ file and thus is not considered a topic worthy of discussion time. Before posting any such information the professional should consult the FAQ file to see what information is already considered common knowledge. If the need arises to mention the information, refer the newbie (first time Interneter) to the FAQ file.

CLIENTS

The Internet offers some potential benefits to clients or patients, too. For example, most professionals have experienced the problem of giving clients written instructions for specific exercises or for care of a piece of equipment. Soon the professional discovers the instructions long ago disappeared never to be found again and the client did not follow the instructions in the first place. So much for the power of the written word! The Internet may provide a solution. Put the instructions on the Internet. For specific clients, the instructions could be sent as an E-mail. To be sure the client received the instructions add the return receipt command to the E-mail. (Instructions for adding the return receipt command to an E-mail are in the manual for the particular E-mail program the professional is using.) Put frequently used instructions on the Gopher or Web page, so clients can refer to them as needed.

The Internet offers a unique way of keeping in touch with clients and families. The professional can send an E-mail on a regular schedule asking the client or family how things are going and if they have any questions or problems. Although such communication could be done by letter, the formalities of writing a letter tend to limit the response. E-mail does not require such formalities. The client can answer with a single word such as "fine" or "great" if there are no problems or keyboard the nature of the problem. There is no need to date the letter, write the return address, write "Dear So and So," end with "Sincerely yours," address the envelope, put on a stamp, and remember to mail it. In addition, the communication is legible because the writing is electronic, not manual. Keyboarding can be done with a mouth stick and even eye gaze. Neither technique is practical for writing on paper. Access to the Internet is also easier to arrange for the person with severe mobility problems. A typewriter loaded with paper is not always within easy reach of the person but a monitor and keyboard can be because the computer can assist with many other tasks (eg, environmental controls). The opportunities for follow-up with clients using the Internet is just beginning to be explored. A creative professional many find many other ways to facilitate communication with clients.

The Internet can also be used as a therapeutic medium. Clients and family members can learn to locate information and answers for themselves. Clients with low motivation may find in the Internet a new world of interest. The Internet proves many opportunities for improvement in fine motor skills, cognitive tasks, and limited types of social interaction. Cognitive skills are probably the strong suit of the Internet. There are many opportunities for memory tasks, problem solving, attending behaviors, and new learning. The opportunities depend on the combined creative efforts of the professional and the client. There are endless groups of games to play, groups to join, places to see, and sounds to hear. In addition there are books and magazines to read about all aspects of the Internet. Helping clients join a newsgroup or chat group may become standard therapy for many therapists to suggest.

Right now doing therapy via the Internet is just beginning to be possible but medicine is already working the techniques. With telemedicine, radiographs can be viewed directly from the originating site and pressure-sensitive gloves can provide feedback regarding lumps and bumps on a person's body. Videoconferencing may provide information with which to assess a person's strengths and weaknesses. Initial therapy instructions can then be given to trained personnel based on remote viewing and analyzing of a client or patient. Soon therapists will be able to treat or provide consultation for treatment from many miles away without having to physically visit the site where the client or patient is located. This arrangement may help solve the problem of providing quality services to rural areas.

PROFESSIONAL

The Internet offers some real advantages to busy practitioners. Many services can be provided over the Internet. The Listservs, newsgroups, and chat groups offer direct sources of colleague interaction to ask questions, provide factual data, and give suggestions for techniques and approaches to therapy for clients whose problems are not easily solved. Therapists can have the benefit of many other therapists' knowledge without ever leaving the office or clinic.

The opportunities for continuing education are even greater. The Internet offers the chance to learn from the best minds in the field with no travel or time away from home. Although some continuing education may be free, a registration fee is still likely to be the norm. Nevertheless, the convenience should make it much easier for therapists to get the required continuing education hours. Because the Internet works 24 hours a day, even the time factor is at the therapist's control.

Group research could also be facilitated through the Internet. Everyone can learn the protocol for data collection from the same instructor at the same time. Individual checkout is also possible to be sure each member of the data collection process is doing the data collection is the same manner. For example, learning to give the functional independence measure (FIM) would require that the person go to a specific universal resource locator (URL), sign on, view the tape, and take a short quiz in which actual cases have been videotaped for the therapist to evaluate. Performance-based assessment becomes feasible over the Internet. The initial certification examination could include real client cases videotaped for the examination candidates to complete. Cases would not have to be described in words but could actually be seen and heard on a video. It could change both initial and advanced certification examination dramatically.

New and successful protocols could be viewed online so therapists could see and hear how the technique is actually done. New ideas might be more quickly assimilated into the practicing therapy culture. Useful ideas could be quickly transmitted to any therapist who signed onto the Internet site. Questions could be answered within hours instead of days or months. Textbook information could be updated immediately instead of waiting for a new printed edition.

Distance learning via Internet connections could provide educational opportunities at both the entry and advanced levels. Students could take classes without traveling or moving many miles away. Some distance learning is already being done at selected universities and colleges but not specifically over the Internet.

Undoubtedly the Internet can be used in many other ways to provide better health care services and improve education of health care professionals. Opportunities are available for creative minds to enlarge the scope of Internet services.

UNIT II

TYPES OF INTERNET RESOURCES

CHAPTER 7

■■■■■■■■■■■■■■■■■■■■■■■■■■■■■■■■■■■■■■

Electronic Mail and Mailing Lists

ELECTRONIC MAIL

Electronic mail (E-mail) works in a fashion parallel to mail sent through the postal service (Fig. 7-1). An E-mail must have an address to a specific person or computer stating where it is to be sent and a set of procedures to take the message and route it closer and closer to its destination, where it arrives and is read by the recipient. The process can be divided into 10 steps.

First the E-mail is composed on the E-mail program. Some examples of E-mail programs are Eudora (shareware), Eudora Pro (commercial), Claris E-mailer, MCI Mail, and E-Mail Connection. E-mail programs are also available as part of other services and programs such as American Online, Compuserve, Prodigy, Netscape, Quarterdeck, and others. The E-mail program format has four basic requirements:

1. The message must be addressed to the recipient's E-mail address.
2. The writer's E-mail address, that is, a return or "from" address, must be included.
3. A subject line is necessary to state the purpose of the E-mail.
4. The format has a message area where the message is composed.

Figure 7-2 shows an example of the Eudora E-mail program and Figure 7-3 presents an example of a completed E-mail. A description of the most commonly used E-mail programs is included in Table 7-1.

After the E-mail is composed, it is sent by clicking on the button marked SEND. At this point the simple mail transfer protocol (SMTP), which is part of the transfer communication protocol/Internet protocol (TCP/IP) software, divides the E-mail into small packets, addresses each one, and provides instructions as to how the packets should be forwarded. These instructions include how

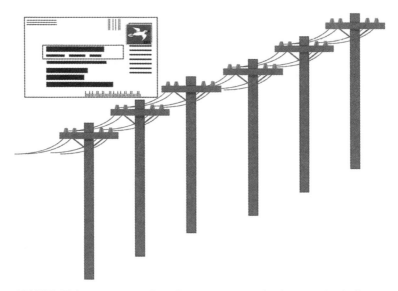

FIGURE 7-1. Sending an E-mail message over the Internet is similar to sending a letter through the postal service.

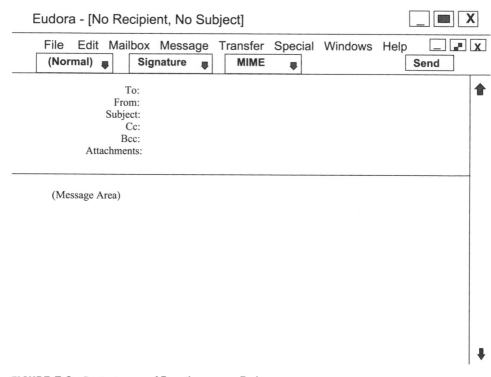

FIGURE 7-2. Basic screen of E-mail program Eudora.

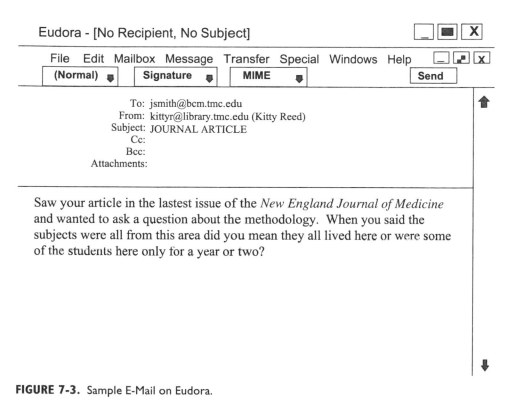

FIGURE 7-3. Sample E-Mail on Eudora.

the packets are to be reassembled at their destinations so the message looks the same as it was composed. The protocol also checks to be sure the message has been received and resends any packet that was lost along the way. If the message is undeliverable, the protocol returns the message to the sender with a note stating it could not be delivered.

Next the message is translated from the computer's digital signal to an analog signal understood by the telephone lines. This is the modem's function: to

TABLE 7-1. COMMON E-MAIL PROGRAMS			
Name	**Source**	**Windows/Mac**	**Full Retail Price**
Eudora Pro 2.2	www.qualcomm.com	Windows/Mac	$80
E-mail Connection 3.0	www.connectsoft.com	Windows	$100
Claris E-mailer 1.	www.claris.com/	Mac	$80
Emissary 1.00	www.twg.com	Windows	$99
NetShart 1.0.4	netshark.inter.net/	Windows/Mac	$39
Pegasus Mail	www.cuslm.ca/pegasus	Windows/Mac	Free
Spry	www.spry.com/	Windows	$80
Quarterdeck Message Center	www.qdeck.com	Windows	$80

modulate and demodulate the signal (Fig. 7-4). This function may soon become unnecessary when all telephone lines are digital.

The fourth step is the message's arrival at a host computer that is already hooked to the Internet. This host computer belongs to the Internet service provider. It may be a local company, a corporation, or a large online service such as America Online.

From the host computer the message goes to a major transfer point called a node. The message may go through several router computers that route the message to the major node (Fig. 7-5). From the major node the message goes out to the Internet over large telephone lines maintained by MCI or Sprint.

The message continues to be transferred from one router to the next while moving ever closer to the destination. These routers also refresh and augment the signal so it can be received in good condition.

Finally, the message reaches the major node closest to the destination and is routed to the host computer, which provides Internet service to the message's recipient.

The recipient's modem translates the message back from an analog to a digital signal. The SMTP program reassembles the message according to the instructions sent with the message and the recipient is notified on his or her E-mail program that a message has arrived. The recipient reads the message.

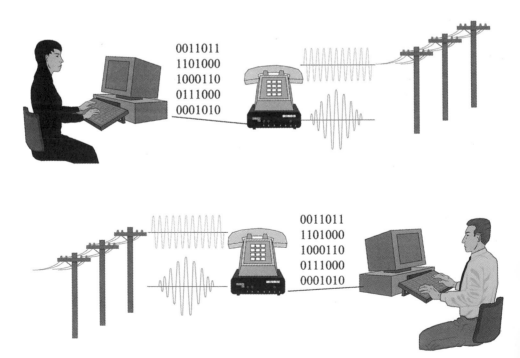

FIGURE 7-4. The computer's digital signal is converted to analog by the modem and sent over the telephone lines where the reverse process occurs at the other end.

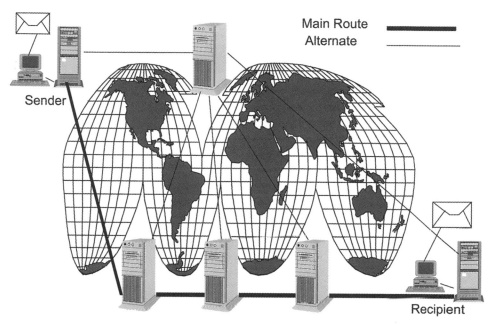

FIGURE 7-5. An E-Mail message traveling on the Internet.

As this discussion illustrates, the address is extremely important. It provides the direction for the message to be sent. An electronic address functions like a postal address, but it is composed differently to accommodate the electronic delivery system. Most electronic addresses are composed of a username or alias that stands for the person's real name. A username is necessary because in computer languages spaces are treated as different entities. Therefore, a person's E-mail address cannot have any spaces in it. The username can be any combination of the person's first and last name or a nickname. Figure 7-6 gives an example. The first author's username is **kittyr**. Note also that the letters are all in lower case, which is common in E-mail addresses. A personal address is always followed by the @ (at) sign. The example now reads **kittyr@**. Next the host computer's name is added, which in the example is library. (A unique name for a library-based computer!) The example reads **kittyr@library**. After the host computer is the subdomain name, if any. A subdomain is not required but often

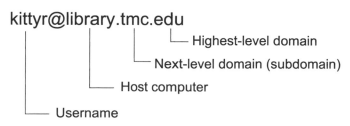

FIGURE 7-6. Analysis of an E-mail address.

appears to provide a unique address. The subdomain and the host computer name are separated by a dot (period). The example reads **kittyr@library.tmc**. The 'tmc' stands for Texas Medical Center. Finally, the domain or group is specified. The complete example reads **kittyr@library.tmc.edu**. The edu stands for education. Some addresses become quite long because of rules within the organization for designating departments or divisions. Long addresses are difficult to type correctly and even more difficult to remember. Given an option, shorter addresses should be used.

Originally the electronic addresses in the United States were divided into six domains. The domains are .edu (education), .org (organization, nonprofit), .com (commercial), .gov (government), .net (network), and .mil (military). Other countries use two-letter codes for domain address. Recently the United States has adopted the international codes for domains that use the country as the domain not the type of institution. The two-letter domain code for the United States is .us. For Canada it is .ca, the United Kingdom is .uk, Australia is .au, Germany is .de, Switzerland is .ch, and so forth (Table 7-2).

TABLE 7-2. INTERNATIONAL DOMAIN CODES	
Domain	**Meaning**
ad	Andorra
ae	United Arab Emirates
af	Afghanistan
ag	Antigua and Barbuda
ai	Anguilla
al	Albania
am	Armenia
an	Netherland Antilles
ao	Angola
aq	Antarctica
ar	Argentina
as	America Samoa
at	Austria
au	Australia
aw	Aruba
az	Azerbaijan
ba	Bosnia-Herzegovina
bb	Barbados
bd	Bangladesh
be	Belgium
bf	Burkina Faso

(continued)

TABLE 7-2. INTERNATIONAL DOMAIN CODES (CONTINUED)

Domain	Meaning
bg	Bulgaria
bh	Bahrain
bi	Burundi
bj	Benin
bm	Bermuda
bn	Brunei Darussalam
bo	Bolivia
br	Brazil
bs	Bahamas
bt	Bhutan
bv	Bouver Island
bw	Botswana
by	Belarus
bz	Belize
ca	Canada
cc	Cocos (Keeling) Islands
cf	Central Africa Republic
cg	Congo
ch	Switzerland ("Cantons of Helvetia")
ci	Ivory Coast
ck	Cook Islands
cl	Chile
cm	Cameroon
cn	China
co	Colombia
cr	Costa Rica
cs	Czechoslovakia
cu	Cuba
cv	Cape Verde
cx	Christmas Island
cy	Cyprus
cz	Czech Republic
de	Germany ("Deutschland")
dj	Djibouti
dk	Denmark
dm	Dominica
do	Dominican Republic
dz	Algeria
ec	Ecuador
ee	Estonia
eg	Egypt

(continued)

TABLE 7-2. INTERNATIONAL DOMAIN CODES (CONTINUED)

Domain	Meaning
eh	Western Sahara
er	Eritrea
es	Spain ("Espana")
et	Ethiopia
fi	Finland
fj	Fiji
fk	Falkland Island (Malvinas)
fm	Micronesia
fo	Faroe Islands
fr	France
fx	France (European Territory)
ga	Gabon
gb	Great Britain (same as uk)
gd	Grenada
ge	Georgia
gf	Guyana (France)
gh	Ghana
gi	Gibraltar
gl	Greenland
gm	Gambia
gn	Guinea
gp	Guadeloupe (France)
gr	Greece
gs	South Georgia and South Sandwich Islands
gt	Guatemala
gu	Guam
gw	Guinea Bissau
gy	Guyana
hk	Hong Kong
hm	Heard & McDonald Island
hn	Honduras
hr	Croatia
ht	Haiti
hu	Hungary
id	Indonesia
ie	Republic of Ireland
il	Israel
in	India
io	British Indian Ocean Territory
iq	Iraq
ir	Iran

(continued)

TABLE 7-2. INTERNATIONAL DOMAIN CODES (CONTINUED)

Domain	Meaning
is	Iceland
it	Italy
jm	Jamaica
jo	Jordan
jp	Japan
ke	Kenya
kg	Kyrgyz Republic
kh	Cambodia
ki	Kiribati
km	Comoros
kn	St. Kitts Nevis & Anguilla
kp	Korea (North)
kr	Korea (South)
kw	Kuwait
ky	Cayman Islands
kz	Kazachstan
lb	Lebanon
lc	Saint Lucia
li	Liechtenstein
lk	Sri Lanka
lr	Liberia
ls	Lesotho
lt	Lithusania
lt	Lithuania
lu	Luxembourg
lv	Latvia
ly	Libya
ma	Morocco
mc	Monaco
md	Moldavis
mg	Madagascar (Republic of)
mh	Marshall Islands
mk	Macedonia
ml	Mali
mm	Myanmar
mn	Mongolia
mo	Macau
mp	Northern Mariana Island
mq	Martinique (France)
mr	Mauritania
ms	Montserrat

(continued)

TABLE 7-2. INTERNATIONAL DOMAIN CODES (CONTINUED)

Domain	Meaning
mt	Malta
mu	Mauritius
mv	Maldives
mw	Malawi
mx	Mexico
my	Malaysia
mz	Mozambique
na	Namibia
nc	New Caledonia (France)
ne	Niger
nf	Norfolk Island
ng	Nigeria
ni	Nicaragua
nl	Netherlands
no	Norway
np	Nepal
nr	Nauru
nu	Niue
nz	New Zealand
om	Oman
pa	Panama
pe	Peru
pf	Polynesia (France)
pg	Papua New Guinea
ph	Philippines
pk	Pakistan
pl	Poland
pm	St. Pierre & Miquelon
pn	Pitcairn
pr	Puerto Rico
pt	Portugal
pw	Palau
py	Paraguay
qa	Qatar
re	Reunion (France)
ro	Romania
ru	Russian Federation
rw	Rwanda
sa	Saudi Arabia
sb	Solomon Islands
sc	Seychelles

(continued)

TABLE 7-2. INTERNATIONAL DOMAIN CODES (CONTINUED)	
Domain	**Meaning**
sd	Sudan
se	Sweden
sg	Singapore
sh	St. Helena
si	Slovenia
sj	Svalbard & Jan Mayen Islands
sk	Slovakia (Slovak Republic)
sl	Sierra Leone
sm	San Marino
sn	Senegal
so	Somalia
sr	Suriname
st	St. Tome & Principe
su	Soviet Union
sv	El Salvador
sy	Syria
sz	Swaziland
tc	Turks & Caicos Islands
td	Chad
tf	French Southern Territory
tg	Togo
th	Thailand
tj	Tadjikistan
tk	Tokelau
tm	Turkmenistan
tn	Tunisia
to	Tongo
tp	East Timor
tr	Turkey
tt	Trinidad & Tobago
tv	Tuvalu
tw	Taiwan
tz	Tanzania
ua	Ukraine
ug	Uganda
uk	United Kingdom
um	US Minor outlying island
us	United States
uy	Uruguay
uz	Uzbekistan
va	Vatican City State

(continued)

TABLE 7-2. INTERNATIONAL DOMAIN CODES (CONTINUED)

Domain	Meaning
vc	St. Vincent & Grenadines
ve	Venezuela
vg	Virgin Islands (British)
vg	Virgin Islands (United States)
vn	Vietnam
vu	Vanuatu
wf	Wallis & Futuna Islands
ws	Samoa
ye	Yemen
yt	Mayotte
yu	Yugoslavia
za	South Africa
zm	Zambia
zr	Zaire
zw	Zimbabwe

Within an institution or company it is not necessary to use the full E-mail address. Usually only the username is required because the host computer and domain are the same for everyone. For example, all employees at the Texas Medical Center Library have the same designation after the sign. Only the username is different. Some organizations are large enough to have more than one host computer. In this case the username and the host computer's name would be necessary to send an E-mail to a coworker whose address is on the other host computer.

Some tips on using E-mail:

1. Keep a list of E-mail addresses. Most E-mail programs provide a means of keeping the E-mail addresses in the program. Putting them in the computer address book eliminates little piles of paper with addresses, which quickly grow into a huge pile where everything important gets lost.

2. Empty the E-mail inbox regularly (Fig. 7-7). Create file folders in the E-mail program to save important messages and delete the rest. Some E-mail programs and Internet service providers provide only so much computer storage space for E-mail for each person. If the space is exceeded, the messages never get delivered. There is no central post office to hold the excess mail until it is picked up or delivered at a later date.

3. Add the E-mail address to the personal business card. Ask friends or business acquaintances to write their E-mail addresses on their business cards if not already present.

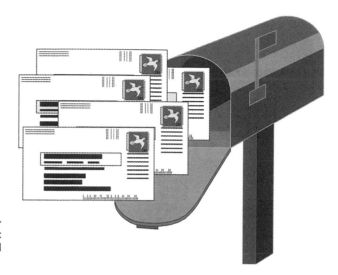

FIGURE 7-7. Remember to delete old E-mails. The electronic space can fill up just like a postal box can.

4. Add the E-mail address to the official letterhead on business stationery.
5. The computer can be instructed to collect and send E-mail responses at a time when the telephone rates are lower. Consider downloading incoming messages and batching outgoing responses together at a nonpeak time to save money.

MAILING LISTS

Mailing lists are discussion groups composed of people with a common interest, all of whom receive the same E-mail that has been posted in a list (Fig. 7-8).

Mailing lists are usually more specialized than newsgroups, which are discussed in the next chapter. Also mailing lists are designed to send the messages directly to the subscriber's E-mail address, whereas the user must access the newsgroup each time to read the latest postings. Nothing comes to recipients to alert them that new messages have been posted on the newsgroup.

The three major types of mail servers on the Internet are Listserv, Listproc, and Majordomo. Listserv, short for list server, was originally written at IBM to run on IBM mainframes. The current version was written by Eric Thomas at L-Soft International and is a commercial program. Listproc or ListProcessor was written by Anastasios Kotsikonas at Boston University. Majordomo was written by Brent Chapman who owns the Internet security consulting company Great Circle Association. Two lesser used programs are Mailbase and Mailserv.

There are many, many mailing lists. Just getting a list of the lists is a challenge. For a list of Listservs send an E-mail message to **listserv@listserv.net** and in the message field type *list global*. The E-mail will probably come back in more than 10

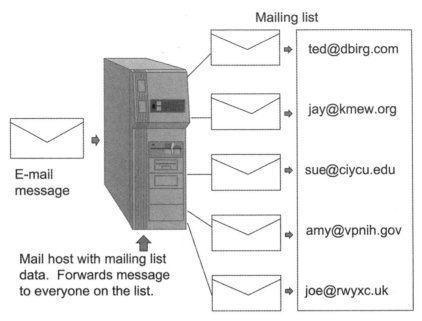

FIGURE 7-8. How a Listserv works.

E-mail messages because of the size. To reduce the number, type a subject after the word list such as *list global/therapy*. The list is also available at **http://tile.net/list-serv/**. Another very large list is available at **mail-server@nisc.sri.com**; in the message field, type **send netinfo/interest-groups**.

Mailing lists have two E-mail addresses: one for subscriptions or requests and the other for messages to be distributed to the list, called the list address. To subscribe to a list, it is important to know whether the list is managed by a person or by a computer. If a person manages the list a request to subscribe must be addressed to the person using the word -request at the end of the username before the sign. For example, if the list is about *splints* and it is managed by a person at *Rehab University* the request to subscribe would be sent to **splints-request@venus.ru.edu**. The list address would be **splints@venus.ru.edu**. If a computer program manages the list, the request address is the same as the list address, except the computer program name is used in place of the username. Using the previous example, the request address is **listserv@venus.ru.edu**, **listproc@venus.ru.edu**, or **majordomo@venus.ru.edu**; the list address is still **splints@venus.ru.edu**.

Although the distribution of E-mail is basically the same for each program, the details of subscribing, unsubscribing, stopping mail temporarily, and getting a list of subscribers varies slightly. Below are the common commands.

Subscribe to a list:
Listserv: In the message area type *subscribe listname yourname*.
Listproc: In the message area type *subscribe listname yourname*.

Majordomo: In the message area type *subscribe listname*. (Note: The program will locate your name and E-mail address from the E-mail header.)

Unsubscribe to a list:
Listserv: In the message area type *signoff listname*.
Listproc: In the message area type *signoff listname* or *unsubscribe listname*.
Majordomo: In the message area type *unsubscribe listname*.

Get help about the commands:
Listserv: In the message area type *help* or *info refcard*.
Listproc: In the message area type *help*.
Majordomo: In the message area type *help*.

Stop mail temporarily:
Listserv: In the message area type *set listname nomail*. To restart type *set listname mail*.
Listproc: In the message area type *set listname mail postpone*. To restart type *set listname back*.
Majordomo: No command available to temporarily stop or restart mail.

Get list of subscribers:
Listserv: In the message area type *review listname*.
Listproc: In the message area type *recipients listname*.
Majordomo: In the message area type *who listname*.

CHAPTER 8

■■■■■■■■■■■■■■■■■■■■■■■■■■■■■■■■■■■

Newsgroups

Newsgroups are electronic public posting sessions on every subject that can be discussed using words. Most newsgroups are not really about current news stories but about subjects of interest to a group of people. Newsgroups also are not true Internet services because they do not require transmission control protocol/Internet protocol (TCP/IP) software to operate. Nevertheless newsgroups are a popular communication format on the Internet.

Newsgroups are usually called Usenets. Usenet is short for user network. The network is divided into seven major hierarchies or categories, plus many add-ons. The big seven are comp., misc., news., rec., sci., soc., and talk. Comp. groups discuss computers, hardware, and software. Misc. groups discuss miscellaneous subjects and act as classified ads. News. groups usually discuss issues related to Usenets or provide information such as lists and announcements about Usenets. Rec. covers recreational topics such as sports, arts, crafts, cooking, and food. Sci. discusses scientific, medical, and physics topics. Soc. subjects include sociology and cultural topics. Talk. topics cover a variety of subjects. Usenets that adopt one of the big seven topical headings are most carefully controlled.

The add-ons include alt. (alternative), bionet. (biology), bit. (bitnet), biz. (business), gnu. (free software), ieee (Institute of Electrical and Electronic Engineering), info. (Information), k12. (education), vmsnet (Vax mainframes), and others as approved. New ones must be approved by the Usenet community before they can be added to the list. The new groups are not as closely controlled as are the original groups. In addition to the national groups, numerous regional groups discuss a wide variety of subjects, such as topics related to California or New York.

Beyond the major headings are a number of divisions. Thus the comp. discussion groups include comp.database, comp.graphics, comp.lang. comp.mac, and many more. In turn each of these groups is subdivided.

Although anyone can start a group, an accepted etiquette is used. Instructions are posted periodically. The best way to become familiar with the Usenet guidelines is to read the group called news.announce.newusers, which provides general information about the Usenet.

To access Usenet the user must have the network news transfer protocol (NNTP) available in the Internet browser or as a separate file. Many of the available newsreaders include the NNTP files. Some Internet browsers such as Netscape have a newsreader with NNTP built into the program. However, there are many choices if one is not available. For Unix machines the best known programs are rn (Read News), trn (Threaded Read News), nn (No News is Good News), and tin (Threaded Internet Newsreader). Windows-based newsreaders include News Xpress, WinTrumpet, and WinVN. WinVN is a public domain software and can be used by anyone. It is available via anonymous file transfer protocol (FTP) from ftp.ksc.nasa.gov in the /pub/winvn/win3 directory.

Some newsreaders are designed to permit offline reading of messages. The messages are downloaded and then read after the online connection is terminated. For users paying by the hour, downloading can save money or free time for other online activities. Two offline readers are available. Free Agent is available via anonymous FTP from ftp.fortein.com in the /pub/agent/ directory. New versions are being added frequently so download the latest one. WinQVT by QPC Software is actually a suite of programs that includes a newsreader, mail program, Telnet, and FTP. WinQVT is a shareware program. The FTP site is listed in Display 8-1. Both 16- and 32-bit formats are available. Registration is $40.

Although each program operates slightly differently, the major functions are similar. First the user must subscribe by selecting among the 6,000 groups. To read the messages in a group, select the group and the message will display. After reading the first message use the forward command to move to the next. To reply select the reply command. To copy a message select and open the message and then select the mail command. To post a message use the post command.

Display 8-1. NEWSGROUP PROGRAMS

Free Agent (Windows)	ftp://ftp.forteinc.com/pub/forte/
Netscape (Win, Mac)	Commercial
NewsBin (Windows)	ftp://ftp.enterprise.net/pub/mirrow/winsock-1/
Newswatcher (Mac)	ftp://ftp.acns.nwu.edu/pub/newswatcher
News Xpress (Windows)	ftp://ftp.hk.super.net/pub
Smart NewsReader (Windows)	http://www.intel.com/iaweb/aplets/
WinQVT (Windows)	ftp.cica.indiana.edu/pub/pc/win3/winsock
WinTrumpet (Windows)	ftp.trumpet.com.au
WinVN (Windows)	ftp.ksc.nasa.gov

The user should be aware of the etiquette regarding the particular Usenet before posting messages. Some groups are information only. Discussion is for the purposes of clarification only. Groups with *announce* in the name are examples of information only groups. Other groups are organized to discuss differing points of view and disagreement is expected. Read some messages and lurk for a while before posting a message.

The user should also be aware that some groups are moderated and some are not. Moderated groups have an administrator who controls what is posted. If the message is not within the subject scope of the group, the moderator may not post it. If the message is too inflammatory, the moderator may elect not to post it. Other groups have no designated moderator and anything sent to the group is posted. Flame wars (see Chapter 10) can be common in such groups when the purpose is to discuss differing views. The user may find the language offensive, ugly, and in bad taste. The best approach is to find another group. Democracy in action is not necessarily all sweetness and light.

CHAPTER 9

■■■■■■■■■■■■■■■■■■■■■■■■■■■■■■■■■■■

Internet Relay Chat and Chat Rooms

Chatting in real time allows the user to "talk" with one or more than one person at a time. "Talking" is actually done by typing rather than by telephone (Figs. 9-1 and 9-2). Internet Relay Chat (IRC) requires a separate client program designed for IRC. The client program can be free standing or be part of a suite of programs designed for Internet access. Chat rooms, on the other hand, are offered by all major online services including America Online (AOL) and CompuServe.

One of the oldest general IRCs is Efnet (http://irc.ucdavis.edu/efnet/). It links 100 servers together to connect 11,000 users. Another IRC group is the UnderNet (http://irc.ucdavis.edu/undernet/), which links 27 servers and about 3,000 people. A third group is the DALnet (http://irc.ucdavis.edu/dalnet/), which started as a role-playing game. It links 16 servers.

IRC was designed by Jarkko Oikarinen in Finland (jto@tolsun.oulu.fi) as an alternative to Talk, which is a one-on-one protocol run from the Unix command line. Started in 1988, IRC is used all over the world with thousands of people logging on every day. The major difference between IRC and chat rooms is that IRC is free, whereas chat rooms are part of a paid monthly service. Also IRCs are unsupervised and unregulated, whereas most chat rooms are moderated.

There are two ways to connect to an IRC. Both require an Internet service provider. One way is through a text-only Unix shell account operated through a program such as Terminal on Windows 3.1 or HyperTerminal on Windows 95. The second is through point-to-point protocol (PPP) or serial line interface protocol (SLIP) using an IRC client program such as mIRC. A PPP or SLIP allows the user to connect to the Internet itself rather than through a host computer and issuing commands through the shell account.

The latest version of mIRC by Khaled Mardam-Bey is designed for Windows 95. To check other software client programs options and read reviews about other clients go to http://www.irchelp.org/.

Dick. "Hi, how are you?"
Jane. "I'm fine, and you?"
Dick. "Doing good."
Jane. "Enjoying your new
    computer?"
Dick. "You bet. It's great."

FIGURE 9-1. Telephone conversation in real time.

Basic commands include:

1. Choose a nickname by typing /nick and then type your nickname.
2. View the list of current channels by typing /list.
3. Join a channel by typing /join and the name of the channel. Note that most channels have a pound or number sign (#) in front of their name.

Display 9-1 is a list of the major commands used on IRCs.

Remember to mind your manners. Type at a rate that permits reasonably accurate spelling. Correct spelling is more important than blazing speed. Remember the hare and tortoise (Fig. 9-3). To correct a typo, retype the error, plus an = (equal) sign and corrected word. For example, speeling = spelling. Another good manner is to join a group with "Hello" and then watch the conversation for a few minutes before joining.

A number of phrases have been used so many times that frequent chatters have developed shorthand versions using the first letter of each word. Display 9-2 summarizes ones that are commonly used. Other conventions have been adopted to express emotions called "smileys" or emoticons. Display 9-3 lists some of the common emoticons.

Be aware that although many people are honest and well intentioned in their conversation, a few are not. If the story sounds to good to be true, it probably is not. Some people feel free to be what they are not when the keyboard is the ma-

dick>hi. how are you?
jane>i'm fine, and you?
dick>doing good.
jane>enjoying your new
    computer?
dick>you bet! it's great.

FIGURE 9-2. Internet relay chat in real time.

DISPLAY 9-1. MAJOR COMMANDS ON INTERNET RELAY CHAT

/ (plus the first letter of a possible command)—shows all the commands that start with that letter

/away (plus a message)—leaves a message saying the user has left the screen for some reason. Example, /away to answer doorbell.

/help—prints help on the given command

/ignore (plus a nickname)—removes output from specific person from the user's screen

/join (plus channel name)—allows a person to join a channel

/leave—leave a channel

/list—lists channels, number of users, and topics

/me (plus a message)—sends a message to the channel that tells what the user is doing. For example, typing

/me eating a sandwich would appear as "(Nickname) eating sandwich."

/msg (plus nickname, plus message)—sends a private message to the nickname of the person the user wishes to reach. Only that person will see the message.

/names—shows the nicknames of the users on the channel

/nick (plus the user's nickname)—changes the user's nickname

/notify (plus a nickname)—notifies the user when the person with that nickname logs in or out of the IRC

/query (plus a nickname)—starts a private conversation with the person the user names. To end a private conversation type /query with nothing after it.

/quit—exits the IRC session

/topic (plus a new topic)—changes the topic of a channel

/who—displays the nicknames of the people on a channel

/whois (plus a nickname)—displays information about the person behind the nickname

jor communication instrument. Also note that many channels have raunchy titles and equally raunchy content. If off-color jokes and sexually oriented content is not interesting to you, find another channel. In addition, do not be intimidated or harassed. Do not follow any instructions that are not clearly understood and terminate any conversation that is getting uncomfortable.

America Online allows up to 23 people to talk together in one chat room. If more join, a second chat room is opened. There are three basic types of chat rooms: public rooms, member rooms, and private rooms. Public rooms are permanent rooms that AOL has established to address members' interests. Member rooms are temporary public rooms that members create to discuss a topic that is not on the list of permanent rooms. Private rooms are temporary rooms that members can create to talk privately with one person or a few people.

All rooms are entered through the People Connection or by selecting Lobby from the Go To menu. The Lobby itself is a chat room and a message will appear to state which lobby the person is in, such as ***You are in "Lobby 21"***. To start a conversation type a message such as "Hello everyone" and click the Send

FIGURE 9-3. One types too fast and the other types too slow.

button in the right bottom of the screen. The message is typed in a box at the bottom of the screen but appears in the middle of the screen with other messages. Someone in the lobby will reply, perhaps several people, with a message acknowledging the individual, say "Hi [your alias][their alias]." If the screen name starts with "Guide," that person is available to help others in the chat room or direct users to other chat room opportunities. Read the screen to see what, if any, conversation is in progress and join in the topic.

DISPLAY 9-2. COMMON ACRONYMS USED BY CHAT GROUP MEMBERS

AFAIK
As far as I know

AFK
Away from keyboard

B4N
Bye for now

BCNU
Be seeing you!

BOF
Birds of a feather. People interested in the same topic who flock together.

BRB
Be right back

BTW
By the way

CUL
See you later

(continued)

DISPLAY 9-2. COMMON ACRONYMS USED BY CHAT GROUP MEMBERS (CONTINUED)

FAQ
Frequently asked questions

FOF
Friend of a friend. A distant and possibly unreliable source.

FWTW
For what it's worth

<G>
Grin

GAL
Get a life

GIGO
Garbage in, garbage out. From computer speak meaning if the input data is wrong the report will be wrong.

GIWIST
Gee, I wish I'd said that

GMTA
Great minds think alike

HHOK
Ho ho only kidding. Just a joke.

HHOS
Ha ha only serious. Half funny and half serious.

IKWUM
I know what you mean

IME
In my exerience

IMHO
In my humble opinion

IMO
In my opinion

IOW
In other words

IRL
In real life

IWBNI
It would be nice if.

YFEG
Insert your favorite ethnic group. Allows user to insert the ethnic group to avoid offending anyone on the newsgroup or chat line.

(continued)

DISPLAY 9-2. COMMON ACRONYMS USED BY CHAT GROUP MEMBERS
(CONTINUED)

JIC
Just in case

LJBF
Let's just be friends

LOL
Laughing out loud

LTNS
Long time no see.

MEGO
My eyes glaze over. Used to mean the person does not understand the technical details or is bored with it.

MOTAS
Member of the appropriate sex

MOTOS
Member of the opposite sex

MOTSS
Member of the same sex

MTC
My two cents

NBIF
No basis in fact

OHDH
Old habits die hard

PMJI
Pardon my jumping in.

POMKIF
Pounding on my keyboard in frustration. Learn how to type!

ROTFL
Rolling on the floor laughing. It was really funny.

RTFAQ
Reading the frequently asked questions. Read the FAQ file before asking a question.

RTFM
Read the "Friendly or f***ing" manual. Don't ask questions that are answered in the manual.

RTM
Read the manual. Read the instructions before asking the question online.

<S>
Smile

(continued)

DISPLAY 9-2. COMMON ACRONYMS USED BY CHAT GROUP MEMBERS (CONTINUED)

SO
Significant other

TIA
Thanks in advance

TTFN
TaTa for now!

WOMBAT
Waste of money, brains, and time

WRT
With respect to

YMMV
Your mileage may vary. You may not get the same result.

For more acronyms see Tamosaitis, N. (1994). *net.talk*. Emeryville, CA: Ziff-Davis Press.

To see what else is going on, click on the List Rooms button. The PC Studio button provides access to information about what is happening that week and also provides a list of acronyms called online shorthands if the user wants additional items not listed in Displays 9-2 or 9-3. The Chat Preferences button allows the user to customize the chat session by specifying who the user wants to talk to and about what. The Parental Control button allows parents to keep children from visiting certain chat rooms the parent prefers the children not visit. Center

DISPLAY 9-3. SMILEYS OR EMOTICONS

O:-)
Angel

(:-&
Angry

:-c
Bummed out

:-#
Censored

:*)
Clowning around

:'-(
Crying

(continued)

DISPLAY 9-3. SMILEYS OR EMOTICONS (CONTINUED)

>:- >
Devilish

:-e
Disappointed

<-|
Dunce

:-!
Foot in mouth

~=
Flaming

:-(
Frowning

||*(
Handshake offered

||*)
Handshake accepted

:->
Happy

:'->
Happy and crying

[ ]
Hug (put name of person between square brackets)

:-S
Incoherent

:-|
Indifferent

:-x
Kiss

>:-<
Mad or angry

:/
Not funny

:-$
Put your money where your mouth is

(:-)
Sad

:-D
Said with a smile

(continued)

DISPLAY 9-3. SMILEYS OR EMOTICONS (CONTINUED)

:->
Sarcastic

:-@
Screaming

%-}
Silly

:-/
Skeptical

:-)
Smile

. . .---. . .
SOS

:-o
Surprised

:-J
Tongue in cheek

:-&
Tongue tied

:-0
Uh Oh

:-\
Undecided

{{ }}
Warm fuzzy hug (put name of person between curly brackets)

:@
What!?

;-)
Winking. Also '-)

|-P
Yuk

Tamosaitis, N. (1994). net.talk. Emeryville, CA: Ziff-Davis Press.

Stage is a special type of chat room that provides auditoriums to present special guests or game shows for members to play.

There is a chat room called Occupational Therapy Networking on AOL. It meets on Monday nights from 9:00 to 10:00 Eastern Standard Time. Members can access this forum from the Health Conference Room Menu. Use *Pen* or *Better Health* as keywords to connect.

CHAPTER 10

■■■■■■■■■■■■■■■■■■■■■■■■■■■■■■■■■

Netiquette

Netiquette is a set of guidelines to facilitate use of the Internet for everyone. The guidelines promote socially responsible conduct so that everyone has a chance to use the resources available on the Internet and everyone is treated with respect. Many of the guidelines pertain primarily to E-mail, mailing groups, and newsgroups, but some pertain to all aspects of using the Internet.

1. Read before posting. Reading messages but not participating in the discussion is called lurking. Lurking is an accepted approach to become familiar with the discussion group modus operandi.
2. Read the frequently asked questions (FAQ) file before asking a question (Fig. 10-1). In other words, spare experienced users from having to repeat the answers to questions that have been asked many times before.
3. Always keep your cool. Avoid sending derogatory messages that imply the other person has a low-functioning intelligence (idiot, dumbbell, moron, dunce). Avoid using swear words and offensive language. Avoid personal attacks. When in doubt, wait 24 hours before answering.
4. Avoid flame wars (Fig. 10-2). Do not start a flame war by responding without thinking of the consequences of one's actions and do not continue a flame war if one is already started. Flame wars ruin the Internet for everyone.
5. Use humor carefully. The written word does not always convey the full meaning of humor. Humor relies as much on body language and the timing of presentation as it does on words. What is funny when two people are conversing face to face may lose much

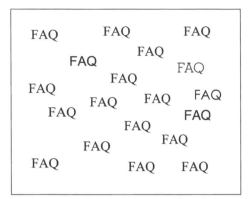

FIGURE 10-1. Always read the FAQs.

of its humor when typed and sent electronically. When in doubt, use simple declarative sentences.

6. Humor can be used if emoticons or smileys are added. Emoticons are small graphic symbols made from typing certain characters on the keyboard together. The most used one is smiley :−) This emoticon means the person is smiling while typing the message.

7. Avoid trolling. Do not post a message that is obviously facetious or ridiculous and do not respond to such a message. There are many examples: Do not respond to a message that says Congress is going to charge a tax on everyone who uses the Internet. Congress is not debating such a tax. Do not send business cards to a child who is dying of an incurable brain tumor. The child has been operated on, is now well, and has grown to adulthood.

8. Avoid cascading. Cascading occurs when someone decides to get in the last word. The posted messages go on and on but say nothing of importance. Do not start a cascade and do not respond to one once it has been identified.

9. Avoid degrading gossip or comments. Do not send any message that could not be printed in a small hometown newspaper or business newsletter. The Internet is not a secure environment. A message can be read by any systems administrator. The message does not disappear when it is deleted from one terminal. The message re-

FIGURE 10-2. Be a cool netter.

mains in the host computer's memory and can be retrieved. So avoid posting a message in which the boss is described as a numb-skull and an ass. The boss may get a copy of the message. E-mail does not have the protection of mail sent via the postal service. Messages can be read and the content can be used to get the sender fired.

10. Avoid the temptation to cross-post. Do not cross-post messages from one list to another unless there is a definite reason to do so. Endlessly cross-posting is called carpet bombing. Seeing the same message several times is irritating. Mention the posted message and offer to send the message directly to those who indicate they have not seen the message. Do not repost the whole message to all readers.

11. In responding to another message, avoid resending a long original message. Pare down or paraphrase the original message.

12. Avoid using technical language when possible. If a technical term is used be sure to give a brief definition. Also avoid using acronyms unless the meaning of the acronym is also included in the message.

13. TYPING IN ALL CAPITAL LETTERS is considered bad form, rude, and the equivalent to shouting at a person 3 feet away in a quiet room. Emphasis can be accomplished by using asterisks or by underlining.

14. Using fancy formatting (bold type or italics), colored letters, bullets, curly brackets, and tab marks is a waste of effort because the E-mail program sends only basic characters.

15. Keep the message and sentence length short when communicating with people who are not well known to the user. There is less chance of being misunderstood.

16. Be aware that all English is not the same. Sometimes misunderstandings can be averted by an astute writer who recognizes the differences in meaning from one English-speaking country to another. In England an elevator is a lift, an apartment is a flat, a truck is a lorry, a faucet is a tap, the hood of a car is a bonnet, and cars are driven on the left side of the road.

17. Check for spelling errors and typos. E-mail is a quick form of communication, which is both a strength and a weakness. The strength is the ease with which a message can be composed, but the weakness is the tendency to type and send without rereading the message for correct grammar and using a spell checker to check the spelling.

18. Always sign your messages with your name and E-mail address. Including a telephone and fax number can be helpful in case the recipient would prefer another communication method.

19. Do not make or use an elaborate signature that takes up a quarter or more of the monitor to display. Self-glorification is not good form on the Internet.

CHAPTER 11

■■■■■■■■■■■■■■■■■■■■■■■■■■■■■■■■■■■

Archie and ArchiePlex

Archie is the original search tool on the Internet. As the number of computers increased on the Internet during the early 1970s, users found the task of remembering information sources more and more difficult. Too many files, directories, and computer addresses existed even for the experienced user. For new users the discovery process was a daunting task. A more efficient process was needed. Computers are supposed to be good memory tools. Why not create a computer program that would gather the source information together in one place? Alan Emtage, Bill Heerlan, and Peter Deutsch at the McGill University School of Computer Science thought an index or table of contents was a good idea. They had the additional impetus of looking for freeware or shareware sources to save McGill University money. Why pay for software programs when good ones were available free or for a small registration fee?

The Archie software program works by collecting directory information from computer sites around the world. The program is always working to update its information. Most Archie servers have a schedule for updating their directory information. When a user wants information, the user connects to an Archie server, logs in, enters a search term, and waits for Archie to search its data base and provide a list of file names in which the search term appears. Although initially the major role of Archie was to identify software programs, many text files related to computer subjects also exist.

There are several Archie sites (computers running the Archie software) although an up-to-date list is difficult to maintain because missions and directives of computers are changed by their human controllers. Most Archie sites do try to maintain a current list on their computer so that if their computer is too busy, the user can select another site. The old rule of thumb was that a user should try to use the Archie server closest to the user's physical location to conserve Internet resources. That rule quickly became impractical in the United States because nearby Archie sites are busy day and night. A more practical approach is to select an Archie site around the world where the local time is the middle of night when local users were likely to be asleep. (Note: Many computer nerds are night creatures so sometimes even servers halfway around the world are busy.) The best choices of Archie servers are in Europe and the Far East.

Access to Archie servers is available through all Internet servers including E-mail, Telnet, Gopher, an Archie client, and the Web. To access an Archie server through E-mail type archie and an @ sign before the name of the Archie site. For example, to address the Archie server at the Advanced Network & Services in New York type **archie@archie.ans.net**. To access an Archie server using Telnet, the command is **telnet_archie.ans.net**. Through a Gopher site the connection is usually a Telnet session. The login command is **archie**. There are several Archie client programs including WS-Archie for both Windows 3.1 and 95, and fpArchie. Archie clients provide a form that is filled in and sent to an Archie site. On the Web, Archie is renamed ArchiePlex. The major site is **http://web.nexor. co.uk/archie.html**. ArchiePlex will present a request form that the user completes and sends to an Archie site.

The major commands are the same regardless of the format. There are three basic search parameters: **sub**, **subcase**, and **exact**. Sub will retrieve any file or directory name containing the search term within it, regardless of case. For exam-

---

DISPLAY 11-1. OTHER USEFUL ARCHIE COMMANDS

set pager—Tells Archie to return the search results one page (screen) at a time, which allows it to be read. Without the pager command the results go zooming across the screen at a rate faster than Evelyn Wood can read.

set maxhits 25—Tells Archie to return only 25 hits. The number can be set from 1 to 1000. The command is useful to limit the retrieval to a manageable number. Some common search terms can return several hundred files. Usually fewer than 100 is enough. If the user needs more, the search can be repeated.

set mailto kittyr@library.tmc.edu—Tells Archie where to send the results. The address can be any E-mail address. The user should replace the author's E-mail address with his or hers if the search results are to be sent to the user.

find—This command is used to tell Archie to search for subject following the command. Example: find eudora.

list—This command can be used alone to tell Archie to list all sites in the data base. Be careful; the list can be quite long.

help—This command provides assistance while online. **A ?** will provide a list of topics. Type **done** when finished reading.

quit—Type this command to exit from Archie. The commands exit or bye can also be used.

DISPLAY 11-2. SAMPLE SEARCH USING A TELNET CONNECTION

```
telnet archie.ans.net
Trying 147.225.1.10
Connected to archie.ans.net
Escape character is '^]'
    Welcome to Archie.ans.net
login: archie
# Bunyip Information Systems, 1993
# Terminal type set to 'vt100 24 80'.
# 'erase' character is '^?'.
# 'search' (type string) has the value 'sub'.
Archie>_set pager
Archie>_set maxhits 25
Archie>_set mailto klttyr@library.tmc.edu
Archie>_find eudora
# Search type: sub.
# Your queue position: 3
# Estimated time for completion: 03:20
working. . .|
(Results returned)
Archie>_quit
```

---

ple if the search term is **stroke**, the results will also include keystroke. Subcase is case sensitive. If the term is entered as **stroke**, the entries Stroke or STROKE will not be returned because of the capital letters. Exact means the term will be searched exactly as presented. If **stroke** is the search term, using the exact command will eliminate keystroke because it is not an exact match. However, a file called stroke.zip will also be missed because the ending is different. Most experienced searchers suggest starting with the search parameter sub.

It is possible to combine the search approaches. For example, exact_sub tells the Archie program to search for an exact hit but if none is found to try the substring search. If the parameters are exact_subcase, the search begins using the exact strategy but if nothing is found the case sensitive strategy is tried.

Commands on Archie all begin with the set command. Thus, the parameters discussed above are typed set search sub, set search subcase, or set search exact if E-mail or Telnet is used. Archie clients and ArchiePlex only require checking the desired box. Commands commonly used are summarized in Display 11-1. A sample of an Archie session is outlined in Display 11-2.

CHAPTER 12

■■■■■■■■■■■■■■■■■■■■■■■■■■■■■■■■■■■■■■■

File Transfer Protocol and Downloading

File transfer protocol (FTP) is a standard procedure for exchanging files with a remote host computer. The user needs an FTP client that connects to a remote host computer. The host computer may contain a file the user wants to transfer to the user's computer (downloading) or the user may want to send a file to the remote host (uploading). Figure 12-1 shows the process of downloading from an FTP server. The file may be a software program, a text file, a graphics file, or a sound bite. FTP works for all types of files. It can transfer one file or multiple files. In addition, the FTP program can identify the current directory on the remote host, list the files on the directory, change to other directories, and rename or delete files. Figure 12-2 is an outline of how directories, subdirectories, and files are organized on a computer drive.

When the FTP program connects to a remote host, the most common logon is to anonymous FTP to access files in public directories. Some files require a valid account and a special password that the user must obtain in advance. Access with an account number and password is called a full service account. The two types of accounts are illustrated in Figure 12-3.

Anonymous FTP gives anyone in the world access to certain directories on a remote computer. With anonymous FTP the user logs in to a remote computer with the user identification "anonymous" and the password is the user's E-mail address. For example, if the user wants to a download a copy of a file on arthritis, the process might be as follows. From the printout obtained through an Archie search, the choices of sites are:

Host info.umd.edu (128.8.10.29)
Last updated 19:01 28 May 1996
    Location: /inforM/EdRes/Topic/Disability/Events/People
    FILE -rw-rw-r— 16563 bytes 09:00 23 Mar 1995 arthritis-info

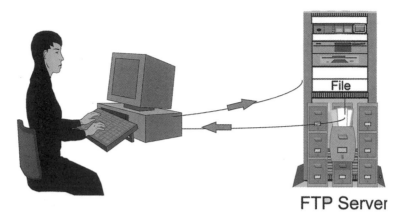

FIGURE 12-1. User requests a file and the FTP server sends that file.

Host zippy.nimh.nim.gov (128.231.98.32)
Last updated 20:21 28 May 1996
   Location: /pub/nih-image/images
   FILE -rw-r—r— 147218 bytes 09:00 8 Oct 1992 arthritis.hqx

Many files available through FTP are text-only format that can be downloaded directly to the user's computer and displayed with a text editor without any special processing. The first file is an example of a text file. However, some files are stored in special formats and need to be processed with special pro-

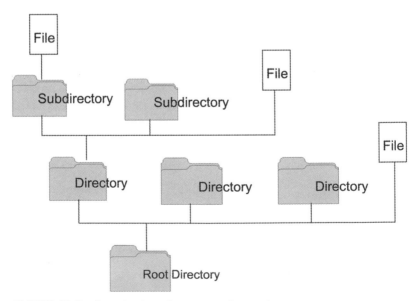

FIGURE 12-2. Organization of computer directories.

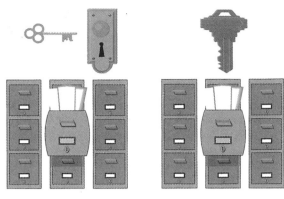

FIGURE 12-3. FTP servers often have two types of files: those available using anonymous login and those requiring a special password.

Public Access
Permitted

Private Access
Must have permission
or an account to use.

grams to be used. Special formats include binary files, compressed files, archived file groups, encoded files, and multimedia formats. The second file is an example of a graphics file that has been compressed with the software program BinHex.

Binary files are nontext files such as computer programs. Binary files must be transferred using FTP binary mode. If the text mode is used, ASCII or EBCDIC for IBM users, the files will be useless. In addition to the binary mode the files are usually compressed or archived, which speeds up the transfer process but requires uncompression or unarchiving before the file is useful. Table 12-1 shows

TABLE 12-1. COMMON COMPRESSION AND ARCHIVAL FORMATS

Extension	Type	Transfer as	Uncompress, Player, or Viewer
.arc	Archive	binary	Uncompress with WinZip
.asc	Text	ascii	Open with word processor
.aif	Sound	binary	Use Wham, Wplany, Netscape Audio
.au	Sound	binary	Use Wham, Wplany, Netscape Audio
.avi	Audio Video Clips	binary	View with Video for Windows or Avi Pro
.bmp	Graphic	binary	View with Bitmap, Lview, PaintShop Pro
.eps	Postscript	ascii	GhostView
.exe	Executable	binary	Execute the file
.gif	Graphic	binary	View with Lview, PaintShop Pro
.gz	Unix Compressed	binary	Uncompress with WinZip
.hqx	Apple, Macintosh	ascii	Convert with BinHex or UNMacKt
.htm	Text	ascii	Open with word processor
.jpg	Graphic	binary	View with Lview, PaintShop Pro

(continued)

TABLE 12-1.   COMMON COMPRESSION AND ARCHIVAL FORMATS (CONTINUED)

Extension	Type	Transfer as	Uncompress, Player, or Viewer
.jpeg	Graphic	binary	View with Lview, PaintShop Pro
.lzh	Lharc Compress	binary	Uncompress with LHA or Winzip
.mpg	Video Clips	binary	Play with MPEGPlay or VMPEG
.mpeg	Video Clips	binary	Play with MPEGPlay or VMPEG
.mov	Video Clips	binary	Play with QuickTime
.pcx	Graphic	binary	Use PC Paintbrush
.ps	Postscript	ascii	Use Adobe Acrobat
.sbi	Sound	binary	Play with Microsoft Sound Blaster
.sit	Macintosh Compressed	binary	Uncompress with UnMacK or Stuffit

some of the common compression and archival formats and the programs used to uncompress or unarchive.

Encoded files are usually files that are prone to file structure damage as they are transferred. Encoding acts as a protection. BinHex is a program used for Macintosh files. Multimedia files include sound, image, and movie formats. The user must have appropriate software and hardware on the computer to play or show these files.

The best FTP program for Windows is WS-FTP. The best source of free or shareware programs is at http://www.tucows.com—select the site closest to your location, then select the operating system, Windows or Macintosh. Select FTP from the list of choices. Via Telnet, FTP software is available from ftp.usma.edu in the /pub/msdos/winsock.files directory or at ftp.cica.indiana.edu in the /pub/pc/win3/winsock/ directory. The best program for Macintosh is Fetch. Other FTP programs are listed in Table 12-2. Some good FTP sites are listed in Table 12-3.

TABLE 12-2.   FTP PROGRAMS FOR MACINTOSH AND WINDOWS

Name of Program	Download from	Type
Anarchie (Mac)	http://www.earthlink.net/nethelp/ mac_apps/fileapps.html	Freeware
CuteFTP (Win 3.x or 95)	http://www.cuteftp.com	Shareware
Fetch (Mac)	http://www.dartmouth.edu/pages/ softdev/fetch.html	Licensed
Integrated Internet File Transfer Protocol Client	www.aquila.com/kent.behrens/	Shareware
NetLoad	http://www.aerosoft.com.au/netload	Shareware
WS-FTP LE 16 or 32-bit (Win)	http://www.csra.net/junodj	Freeware

TABLE 12-3. GOOD FTP SITES IN THE UNITED STATES		
Host Name	**Directory Files**	**Location**
ftp.cica.indiana.edu	/pub/pc/win3/winsock	Indiana
wuarchive.wustl.edu	/system/ibmpc/win3	Missouri
archive.orst.edu	/pub/mirros/ftp.cica.indiana.edu/win3	Oregon
gatekeeper.dec.com	/.t/micro/msdos/win3	California
ftp.cdrom.com	/pub/cica	California
ftp.marcam.com	/win3	Illinois
mrcnext.sco.uiuc.edu	/pub/swn3	Illinois
ftp.dataplex.net	/.1/cica/pc/win3	Texas

CHAPTER 13

■■■■■■■■■■■■■■■■■■■■■■■■■■■■■■■■■■

Telnet

Telnet is one of oldest applications on the Internet. Its beginnings go back to the early 1970s. The term Telnet is short for telephone network. Telnet is actually a terminal emulation program. In other words, it allows the user's computer to act as if it were a keyboard attached directly to another computer that may have a completely different operating system such as Unix. Thus, terminal emulation does three things. First, it allows the user to connect to a host computer that may be many thousands of miles away from the connecting computer without having to pay long distance charges for the telephone line. Second, it allows the user to make the host computer respond as if the keyboard were attached directly to the host. Third, the user gets access to the information on the host computer without having to use any storage memory on the user's computer.

The major reason for connecting to another computer as if it were the user's is to access information on the host computer that is not readily available in another format. Most often the reason for Telneting is to connect to a large data base such as the National Library of Medicine catalog or local medical school library catalog. Other reasons are to access online games, chat groups, or bulletin boards. Another reason is that a Telnet session can be initiated while the user is connected to the Internet using a browser. Thus, the Telnet session can be occurring at the same time using only one telephone line.

To use Telnet, begin the Telnet program and type in the address of the host to be reached. Figures 13-1 and 13-2 show samples of Telnet forms. Figure 13-1 shows a new form to type in a new address. Figure 13-2 shows addresses and names already typed. The user highlights the name of the site and presses enter to activate the connection.

A typical address can be either the numeric or alphabetic address. For example, the address for the National Library of Medicine is **locator.nlm.nih.gov**.

WTNVT ⬇ ⬆

| Session | Edit | Commands | Setting | Help |

⬆

```
┌────────────────────────────────────────────┐
│                    New                     │
├────────────────────────────────────────────┤
│                                            │
│   Host Name or IP Address  ┌────────────┐  │
│                            │            │  │
│                            └────────────┘  │
│                                            │
│  ┌─────────┐ ┌────────┐ ┌────────┐ ┌──────┐│
│  │ Connect │ │  Open  │ │ Cancel │ │ Help ││
│  └─────────┘ └────────┘ └────────┘ └──────┘│
│         ┌──────────────────────┐           │
│         │  Session Parameters  │           │
│         └──────────────────────┘           │
└────────────────────────────────────────────┘
```

Instructions: Type the host name or numeric address
in the box and click on the Connect button.

⬇

FIGURE 13-1. Telnet screen for new entry.

WTNVT ⬇ ⬆

| Session | Edit | Commands | Setting | Help |

⬆

```
┌────────────────────────────────────────────┐
│                    Open                    │
├────────────────────────────────────────────┤
│     Sessions Available                     │
│                            ┌─────────────┐ │
│   ┌──────────────────────┐ │   Connect   │ │
│   │ Medline              │ └─────────────┘ │
│   │ Library Catalog      │ ┌─────────────┐ │
│   │ Archie Server        │ │    Open     │ │
│   │                      │ └─────────────┘ │
│   └──────────────────────┘ ┌─────────────┐ │
│                            │   Cancel    │ │
│                            └─────────────┘ │
│   Host ┌──────────────────┐┌─────────────┐ │
│        └──────────────────┘│    Help     │ │
│   Port ┌──────────────────┐└─────────────┘ │
│        └──────────────────┘                │
└────────────────────────────────────────────┘
```

⬇

FIGURE 13-2. Telnet screen for saved entry.

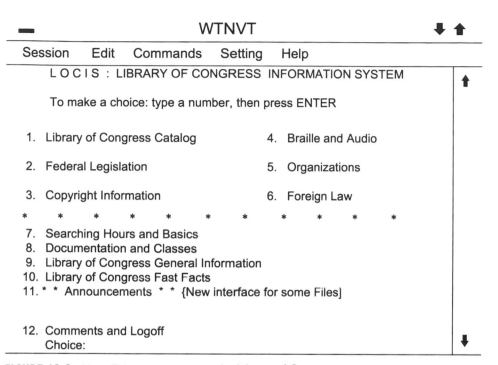

FIGURE 13-3. Using Telnet to connect to the Library of Congress.

When the Telnet connection is complete, the user will be asked to login. The log-in password is *locator*. A menu will appear from which the user can select to search books, titles, and audiovisual items. All items can be selected by typing the highlighted letter. A second menu then appears allowing the exact informa-tion (title or author) to be typed or parts of the title or author. Then a line appears for the search. When the results are displayed to the screen, the user can E-mail one entry or E-mail all the entries back to the user's computer. When the session is completed the user exits and returns to the local computer.

Telnet sites are straightforward. A menu of choices appears on the screen. Follow the instructions and the information is provided. Figure 13-3 illustrates the Library of Congress main screen. The hardest part is often figuring out how to logon and logoff. If there are no instructions on the screen for logon try typing either *guest* or *anonymous*. If a password is required it is usually the user's E-mail address. There are several varieties of logoff commands including quit, exit, end, bye, stop, off, and logoff. Keep trying until one of them works. Another ap-proach is to type h or help? for instructions. Unless the directions say otherwise, assume the computer is case sensitive. Type lower-case letters only.

Several Telnet programs are available. These include COMt, EWAN, NCSA WinTel, Trumpet Telnet, and YAWTel. WinQVT is a combination shareware pro-gram that offers access to Telnet, newsgroups, FTP and E-mail all in one pack-age. Most are available through anonymous FTP. COMt, Trumpet Telnet, and WinQVT are shareware. EWAN, NCSA WinTel, and YAWTel are freeware at

Table 13-1. Telnet Clients Available			
Name and Version	**Rating**	**Location**	**Free or Shareware**
Anzio Lite v.10.9	4	www.teleport.com/~rsi	Shareware
CommNet v.2.1	4.5	www.radient.com	Shareware
CRT v.1.1.2	5	www.vandyke.com/vandyke/crt/	Shareware
Ewan v1.0.52	4	www.ly.sator.liu.se/~zander/ ewan.html	Freeware
MrTerm	3.5	192.216.48.20/mrterm.html	Shareware
NetTerm	5	starbase.neosoft.com/~zkrr01/	Shareware
NCSA Telnet	2.5	www.ncsa.uiuc.edu/SDG/ Software/Brochure/Overview/PC Telnet.overview.html	Freeware
Power VT 1.04	3.5	Not given	Shareware
QVT/Term 4.0.5	4	Not given	Shareware
QWS 3270 v.2.4	3.5	Not given	Shareware
SimpTerm v.0.9.4	4	Not given	Freeware
Trumpet Telnet 2.1	2.5	www.trumpet.com.au	Freeware
UW Term v.0.97g	3	Not given	Freeware
Yawtel v. 0.7 Beta	3.5	Not given	Freeware
WinTelnet v.1.0	4	www.igsnet.com/igs	Shareware

present. Software status and versions can change frequently so always read the instructions before downloading.

America Online has its own Telnet program. It must be downloaded and configured. CompuServe has its Telnet program ready to run by clicking on the Internet icon and selecting the Remote Login button. Netscape does not have a Telnet client packaged in the program. The user needs to download one of the Telnet programs listed above and then under Applications, tell Netscape where to find the program path (name of drive) and the name of file such as c:\ewan.exe.

The Web page, Tucows (no kidding), evaluates the Telnet clients available. A summary is provided in Table 13-1. For the full report, point the browser to http://www.tucows.com. Select the location closest to your computer. Select the format you want, either Windows 3.1, Windows 95, or Macintosh. Click on the listing for Telnet programs and examine the results. Ratings are on a 5-point (cow) scale.

CHAPTER 14

■■■■■■■■■■■■■■■■■■■■■■■■■■■■■■■■■■■■■■

Gopher

Gopher is an Internet browser program that was developed in 1991 after Archie and before the World Wide Web. The first Gopher was developed by the University of Minnesota, home of the golden gopher (Fig. 14-1). The name is variously described as honoring the mascot known for burrowing or tunneling and being a "go fer" program that fetches files or programs of interest to the user (Fig. 14-2). Either way, the Gopher program organizes files into a hierarchy with a numbered list or symbol (Fig. 14-3). Typing the number or clicking on the symbol instructs the program to perform the function and display it to screen (Fig. 14-4). The function may be another directory, a specific file, or instructions to connect to another computer (Telnet). Using the directory function allows the user to go from one topic to another along the same or similar subject.

The Gopher program was created before the wide use of the Windows-based operating system. Originally the files were listed with a number to the left. After Windows was introduced, the numbers were changed to symbols as shown in Figure 14-5. Because both may be seen, it is useful to understand both arrangements. When the files are numbered, the important distinctions are at the end of the line. A file that ends with a forward slash (/) indicates that the entry will lead to another directory list. A file that ends with a dot (.) indicates that the entry will lead to a specific file or document. Another file ending is two arrows with a question mark between them <?> indicating that the entry leads to a data base that can be searched. Sometimes the arrows have the letters <TEL> in between, signifying that the entry leads to a Telnet site such as a library catalog.

When a symbol appears at the beginning of a line, the Windows format is being displayed. Directory files are marked with a graphic of a file folder. Documents are illustrated with a graphic of a page with the upper right hand corner turned down. Binoculars are used to indicate a data base and search server.

Gopher

A small rodent
who likes to
burrow. Oops!
Wrong script.

FIGURE 14-1. A gopher is....

GOPHER

◆ A person who gets things for you. How
about a computer program that gets
things for you?
◆ A client/server application that allows
you to browse large amounts of
information by presenting everything to
the end-user in the form of menus.

FIGURE 14-2. Defining Gopher.

Internet Gopher Information Client 2.0
Root gopher server: gopher.micro.unn.edu

-->1. Information about Gopher/

  2. Computer information/

  3. Internet file server (ftp) sites/

  4. Libraries <TEL>

  5. Search gopher title <?>

  6. Search lots of places <?>

  7. Phone Books/

  8. Fun Stuff

Press ? for Help, q to Quit, u to go up a menu

FIGURE 14-3. Sample Gopher
page.

```
              Internet Gopher Information Client 2.0
              Root Gopher Directory  gopher.unn.edu

          1.  How to use gopher
     -->2.  Gopher commands
          3.  Using Veronica to search directories
          4.  Veronica sites
          5.  Using Jughead to search this directory
          6.  FAQs about gopher
          7.  Gopher jokes
```

FIGURE 14-4. Sample Gopher page continued.

Press ? for help , q for quit, u to go up one menu

Gopher addresses may be stated using their numeral or letter name; the two forms are equivalent. Thus, the following numeric and alphabetic addresses will both reach the library catalog in the Texas Medical Center at Houston: 192.68.30.100 or ils.library.tmc.edu. Most people find the letter format easier to remember. Therefore, addresses are most often listed in the letter format but not always. The important fact is that both will work as long as the domain name server is available to translate the letters into numbers. Occasionally the letter format may not work when the numbers will because the domain name server is not functioning. If neither works three possibilities exist:

1. The host computer is down for repair or not accepting incoming messages due to internal workload.
2. Telecommunications to the host computer are not working.
3. The address has been changed.

Several basic commands are useful in negotiating Gopher. Six key commands are useful—the four arrow keys (right, left, down, up), the space key, and the B key to

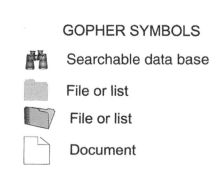

GOPHER SYMBOLS

Searchable data base

File or list

File or list

Document

FIGURE 14-5. Gopher symbols.

```
┌─────────────────────────────────────────────────┐
│            Internet Gopher Information Client 2.0 │
│            Root Gopher Directory gopher.unn.edu   │
│                                                   │
│      ⇓     Move down one line                     │
│      ⇑     Move up one line                       │
│      u     Move back one screen                   │
│      m     Return to main menu                    │
│      /     Search the directory                   │
│    Enter   View item                              │
│      q     quit                                   │
│  Press ? for Help, q to Quit, u to go up a menu   │
└─────────────────────────────────────────────────┘
```

FIGURE 14-6. Gopher commands.

go back. In addition, the question mark is used to display help information about the commands available at any particular point of the Gopher program; the q key is used to quit, followed by the y (yes) or n (no) to confirm; or the upper case Q is used to quit immediately. These plus additional commands are shown in Figure 14-6.

VERONICA

Veronica was developed at the University of Nevada to facilitate searching Gopher sites. The name was selected to follow the characters in the cartoon "Archie" because the first search system was known as Archie (short for Archives). The second search system was named Veronica. Jughead, the third, is discussed later.

Veronica is also an acronym for Very Easy Rodent Oriented Net-wide Index to Computerized Archives. Computer literature is full of computer folklore so one cannot believe everything one reads. Some "facts" are the product of overac-

TABLE 14-1. LOCATION OF USEFUL PUBLIC GOPHERS AND THEIR LOGINS

Location	Telnet to	Log in as
California	infoslug.ucsc.edu	infoslug
University of Illinois	ux1.cso.uiuc.edu	gopher
Michigan State University	gopher.msu.edu	gopher
University of Minnesota	consultant.micr.umn.edu	gopher
Australia	info.anu.edu.au	Info
Japan	gan.ncc.go.ip	gopher
Sweden	gopher.sunet.se	gopher

TABLE 14-2. LOCATING A GOPHER CLIENT PROGRAM		
Name of Program	**File Transfer Protocol Site**	**Ranking**
WSGopher	dewey.tis.inel.gov/pub/wsgopher	Best
Freeware	http://sageftp.inel.gov/dap/gopher.htm	
	wsg-12.exe	
BCGopher	bcinfo.be.edu/PUB/BCGOPHER	Good
Freeware	bcgO8ba3.zip	
Hgopher	ftp.cica.indiana.edu/pub/pc/win3/winsock	Fair
Freeware	hgoph24.zip	
PNLInfo Browser	ftp.pnl.gov/pub/pnlinfo/win	Good
	ib105.exe	
Wgopher	ftp.cuhk.hk/pub/gopher/PC	OK
	wgoph232.exe	

tive imaginations whose owners are either underworked or are taking too many extended breaks.

A Veronica server works by canvassing Gopher site directories and organizing them into a data base that can be searched by any keyword. Those directories containing the keyword are returned to the searcher in the form of a list. The list can be a single page or dozens of pages long. The user then scans the list and selects the Gopher sites to be viewed. Veronica connects the user to that computer.

There are only a few Veronica sites around the world because a computer running the Veronica software will have little hard drive space left for any other computer activity. Keeping track of all the computer directories on the Internet takes enormous computer memory and few people are willing to devote the computer space to such a specific task. There are only about eight Veronica servers in the world and they all keep extremely busy. The best times to use them are early in the morning and late at night.

JUGHEAD

Jughead, the third cartoon character name, is a special form of search engine. It searches only the computer on which it is running. Some computer hosts have gathered a large number of useful documents or data bases onto a single computer or series of computers at a single site. Just searching the directories of the single computer can be time consuming. Enter Jughead, which searches exactly like Veronica. The user enters a keyword to be searched; Jughead searches the directories for matching entries and reports back its findings. The user can then select those directories or documents that are of interest.

Table 14-1 provides the address and login for some useful Gophers to provide a starting point. Table 14-2 lists some Gopher client programs and ranks them according to their useful features.

CHAPTER 15

■■■■■■■■■■■■■■■■■■■■■■■■■■■■■■■■■■

Wide Area Information Server

Wide area information server (WAIS, pronounced ways) is a computer program designed to search full text data bases such as collections of articles, newspapers, electronic textbooks, or Usenet postings. The major difference between WAIS search tools and others such as Veronica and many Web search engines is that WAIS searches the complete contents of documents. Most search tools retrieve information from directories, documents titles, and a few lines at the beginning of the text.

The WAIS program resulted from a joint development project of Thinking Machines Incorporated (a Massachusetts supercomputer company), Apple Computer, Dow Jones, and KPMG Peat Marwick. The project began in the late 1980s and became available on the Internet in 1991. Unfortunately, the timing was not the best. Two factors mediated against wide adoption of the technology. One, WAIS searches the entire document, which requires a large amount of computer memory. As a result, there are not many WAIS servers. The topics available are also limited. In all there about 300 to 500 WAIS servers.

The second factor was the development of the Web, which required less computer memory and offered more flexibility, especially in the multimedia aspects. The Web quickly overshadowed WAIS. Nevertheless, WAIS is an excellent technology and does its job well.

The WAIS program is based on the client-server model. To search a WAIS data base the user must have a WAIS client on the local or host computer. The client program is available from various file transfer protocol (FTP) sites including: ftp.cnidr.org, sunsite.unic.edu, or ftp.wais.com. On the Web a client called WinWAIS is available at ftp://ftp.einet.net/einet/pc. WinWAIS is a shareware program. Registration is $35. If the user has America Online the FTP service available online is recommended because the directions are easy to follow.

Most WAIS servers are available through a Gopher server such as gopher-gw.micro.umn.edu or launchpad.unc.edu. One option on the menu will read "WAIS Based Information/." This option displays a menu of data bases from which to choose. After a data base is selected a search term is entered. The result of the search is a Gopher menu that contains retrieved information.

The WAIS data bases are also available using Telnet. Examples are wais.wais.com or quake.think.com. The login is wais. Two Web sites are http://www.einet.net and http://www.wais.com/newhomepages/waisgate.html, which is the homepage for WAIS Inc. The Usenet newsgroup at comp.infosystems.wais is a good support line for WAIS users.

The WAIS searches are performed using a numerical score that is computed according to how many times the search word or words appear in the document. The score is weighted using a technique called *relevance feedback* so that words found in the title are given a higher score than those in the body of the document. The rationale is that words in the title are more likely to describe the subjects in the document.

When a specific subject is searched the server consults an inverted file, a list of all the significant words (those longer than two letters) in every document in the data base, and computes a score for each. The document with the greatest number of hits (instances of the search subject) is given a score of 1000 and appears at the top of the list of the retrieved documents. Because all search terms are searched, only type the key words to be searched. For example, if the search was for references to the book title *Gone with the Wind*, the search engine would search the words "with" and "the" as well as "gone" and "wind." The results would probably make little sense and may not find much information about the book or anything related to the subject.

THE WORLD WIDE WEB

CHAPTER 16

■■■■■■■■■■■■■■■■■■■■■■■■■■■■■■■■■■■■

The World Wide Web

As the Internet became increasingly popular among educational institutions, professors and students found more creative ways to use it. Dr. Tim Berners-Lee was one of the creators. He developed a program that would let him cross-reference his research papers by using a single highlighted word, called a hyperlink, as a connecting or cross-indexing point from one paper to another. His employer, the European Center for Nuclear Research, soon saw the potential for such a program. Numerous documents could be hyperlinked or hypertexted. In 1991, a demonstration site was put on the Internet to impress fellow scientists. The idea was intriguing but not a real success until 2 years later when the program Mosaic was released.

Mosaic was written at the supercomputing center at the University of Illinois. It was designed to take advantage of the hyperlink and hypertext ideas. In addition, Mosaic provided the first graphic user interface (GUI). The program allowed documents to be interconnected and provided access to sound, video, photographs, animation, and text. Multimedia applications that could include any combinations of text, visual, and sound applications were possible. Mosaic was a huge success. It quickly earned the nickname of a *killer app*, a very successful application program that rapidly becomes the accepted standard. With Mosaic as a launching platform, the World Wide Web became almost synonymous with the Internet. Web sites were created in multitudes and *Information Superhighway* became a household term. The commercial sites realized the advantages immediately. Products could be advertised in ways not possible on television. Consumers could select the way they wanted to look at the product and learn about its attributes. Variety was possible.

Although Mosaic was successful, it was soon eclipsed by an improved program called Netscape, which is the major Web browser or client today. Table 16-1 lists Web browsers available and compares their features. Netscape refined ap-

TABLE 16-1. COMPARISON OF WEB BROWSERS

Name	Location	Price	Rank
Air Mosaic (Win)	http://www.spry.com/order-info.html	$29.95	Good
	Available at most computer stores.		
Cello (Win)	ftp.law.cornell.edu in the /publ/LII/Cello	Free	Fair
	directory		
DosLynx (DOS)	ftp2.cc.ukans.edu in the	Free	Poor, no
	/pub/WWW/DosLynx		graphics
Enhanced NSCA	Luckman Interactive (800)500-4411	$49.95	Good
Mosaic (Mac, Win)			
InternetWorks (Win)	ftp.booklink.com	Free	Very good
MacWeb/Win Web	ftp.einet.net in the /einet/mac/macweb	Free	Mac—good
	ftp.einet.net in the /einet pc/winweb		Win—fair
NCSA Mosaic	ftp.ncsa.uiuc.edu in the Web/Mosaic	Free	Fair
Netscape Navigator	ftp.mcom.com/Netscape. Available at	Share	Best
(Mac & Win)	most computer stores.	$39	
Samba (Mac)	ftp.w3.org in the	Free	Poor
	/pub/www/bin/mac/old		
SlipKnot (Win)	ftp.netcom.com in the	Share	Good
	/pub/pbrooks/slipknot	$39	

plications in Mosaic and made printing easy; all the user needed to do was to click the print button. The growth of Web pages continues. Creative Web page designers find new ways to present information in an interesting, appealing manner.

The popularity of the Web is due in part to the ease of using the Web browsers. There are no commands to remember and implement. Everything is see, point, and click. The buttons are clearly marked as to their purpose. A new user can be surfing the net in a manner of minutes.

The Web works because of the programming language called hypertext markup language, abbreviated HTML or HML. HTML permits the address of one Web page to be embedded in another through the hypertext link. Although the user clicks on a word, symbol, or picture, the command is translated into the address of another Web page.

The address of a Web page is called a uniform resource locator or URL. A URL always contains a colon and two forward slashes. The following are examples of URLs appearing in Web pages: http://, gopher://, telnet://, or ftp://. Http stands for hypertext transfer protocol. It is the protocol used to transfer Web pages over the Internet. Gopher:// is a Gopher site that has been upgraded into a Web page. It will still function like a Gopher page although graphic buttons usually replace the numbered items. Telnet:// is a Telnet site in Web format and ftp:// is a file transfer site in Web format. The advantage to upgrading older formats is that more information and choices can be put on the Web page, reduc-

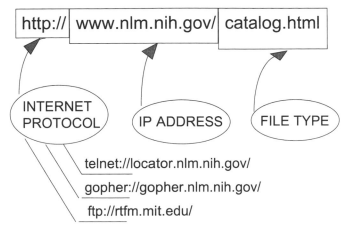

FIGURE 16-1. How to read a universal resource locator.

ing the amount of commands the user must remember and perform without prompts.

Reading a URL is fairly easy. As an example look at Figure 16-1, which diagrams the URL http://www.library.tmc.edu./welcome.html. The http:// means the transfer language is hypertext. The www is bragging to remind everyone this is a Web page. The next code is .library, the name of the host computer, .tmc is a subdomain, and .edu is the domain. The forward slash indicates the end of the actual address. Letters and numbers following the slash are files at that address. Thus **welcome** is a file and .html means the file was written in hypertext markup language.

Chapter 17 explains the Netscape browser in more detail, Chapter 18 provides information about search tools, Chapter 19 explains the error messages, and Chapter 20 discusses the visual and audio potential of the Web. Enjoy the Web and watch out for spiders (Fig. 16.2)!

FIGURE 16-2. Spider webs.

CHAPTER 17

■■■■■■■■■■■■■■■■■■■■■■■■■■■■■■■■■■■■

Netscape Navigator

Netscape Navigator (usually just called Netscape) is generally regarded as the "killer app" of the Web browsers. Figure 17-1 illustrates Netscape's homepage. Netscape is not, however, the only browser. Others are NCSA Mosaic for Windows, NCSA Mosaic for Macintosh, WinWeb, MacWeb, Cello for PCS, Samba for Macs, and Microsoft Internet Explorer. Web browsers can also be found in Internet software suites such as AIR Mosaic in Internet in a Box, Quarterdeck Mosaic in InternetSuite, and Internet Chameleon. All have strengths and weaknesses.

Netscape is being described because of its high profile and because the concepts of other browsers are similar. For educational institutions Netscape is free. It can be downloaded from Netscape's homepage at **http://home.netscape.com/**. For everyone else, Netscape can be purchased online from the homepage and is also available at most computer stores at $40 to $50 for the current upgrade. Older versions sell for $10 to $20 in software surplus catalogs.

To install Netscape follow the basic directions of putting the computer disk in drive A: and typing in the word install. When the program starts tell it which drive to load (c: or d:) and press <Enter>. It will install itself and ask if the user wants to go online. If the answer is yes, the program will sign onto the homepage and provide a list of Internet service providers (ISPs) from which to chose or the user can tell Netscape the IP address of an ISP with which the user already has an account.

Instructions for using Netscape are provided with the program but they are incomplete. More instruction is provided here to guide the user and hopefully reduce frustration. The instructions are for Netscape 2.0 because it is available at the time of writing. Netscape 3.0 may be available when the reader is reading this chapter. Some instructions will not apply. Check the bookstore for an updated copy of the reference listed below or for a similar text.

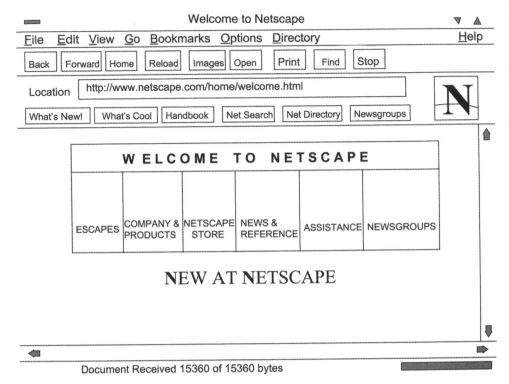

FIGURE 17-1. Outline of Netscape's homepage.

The Netscape screen has buttons, bars, and pulldown menus (Fig. 17-2). The buttons will facilitate most major activities on maneuvering around the Web. The buttons are from left to right: Back, Forward, Home, Reload, Images, Open, Print, Find, and Stop. The Back button takes the user back one screen at a time after the user has left the homepage the first time. The Forward button takes the user forward one screen at a time if the Back button has been used. The Home button will return the user to the homepage immediately, no matter how many screens or Web sites have passed. Home is home. The Reload button is useful when the Web page becomes jumbled and images do not appear that should. The Reload instructs the sending host computer to try sending again and please try to do a better job. The Images button can be ignored unless the user does not want to see the images on the Web pages. The Open button when activated by a click opens a box for the user to type in a universal resource locator (URL) of the user's choice. The Print button enables pages to the printed. That one was easy! Do remember that dot matrix printers cannot reproduce the variety of font sizes and may take a long time to print the graphics. Laser printers are much better for printing out Web pages. The Find button searches for a word or text string (for nonwords) in the Web page currently being viewed. The Stop button stops the loading of a Web.

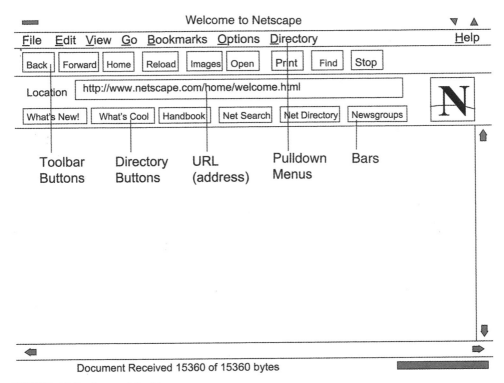

FIGURE 17-2. Parts of the Netscape page.

The bars are What's New, What's Cool, Handbook, Net Search, Net Directory, and Newsgroups. What's New goes to a list of Web pages recently added so the user can check up on new sites that may be of interest. What's Cool goes to a list of novel pages as chosen by the Netscape staff. The user may or may not agree that the choices are "cool." Handbook is the online help book about Netscape. Net Search lists various Internet and Web search tools to assist in locating sites of interest to the user. Net Directory lists various Internet and Web directories that may help the user locate interesting sites. Newsgroups lists the newsgroups to which the user has subscribed.

The pulldown menus include File, Edit, View, Go, Bookmarks, Options, and Directory. The first four provide standard type tools. However, Bookmarks is a little different. Bookmarks allows the user to keep track of URLs that are of interest by marking them so that the URL is stored in Netscape's memory. When the user wants to return to a URL, it can be selected from the stored list and does not have to be typed in again. Bookmarks can be organized into groups of similar types and can be exported as a file for a friend or business acquaintance or Bookmarks can be imported as a file someone gave the user.

The other important pulldown menu is Options. The Options menu is where the user instructs Netscape regarding the choice of homepages (unless the user finds the Netscape homepage irresistible). From the Options menu select Preferences. From the Preferences menu select Appearance. In the first box, check to be sure Show Toolbar is set, and the black circle filled in for Pictures and Text. Next is the Startup box. The black circle should be in the Home Page Location. In the space provided, type in the URL for the homepage of your choice. A good way to select a homepage is to designate one that is frequently useful in locating needed information. Another way is to choose a page that is attractive to view. It will be seen every time the user logs on so it might as well be enjoyable to view.

Below the Startup box is the Link Styles box, which determines how a link is displayed and how long a link stays highlighted (usually hot pink) after it has been visited once. Leave the Underlined box checked. The default for displaying links is 30 days but a longer time period can be selected; the Never Expire circle can be filled in or the Expire Now button can be used to clear anything currently highlighted. Leave the default setting at 30 days unless there is a clear reason to select another choice. Sites that are frequently visited will remain highlighted because the 30 days is figured from the last visit.

Next under Preferences is the Font selection box. The defaults are Latin1 for encoding. It is best to leave the default set as it is for now. Times New Roman is the default for proportional font and Courier New is the default for fixed font. These can be changed but remember that many Web pages are written with these fonts in mind. If they are changed some Web pages may improve in appearance but others will look much worse. Experiment with care or leave them alone.

The third item under Preferences is Color. There are four choices here: Links, Followed Links, Text, and Background. If some color is annoying, change it to another color. If a Web page is hard to read because the Webmaster is either color blind or chose the colors by using the table of random numbers, try changing the text or background to achieve a better contrast. Just remember to change the color back again or all Web pages may begin to look a little weird.

The fourth item pertains to the color choice of images. Netscape can be instructed to automatically choose Web site colors but depending on the resolution of the monitor and the power of the video card some sites may not look their best. The next choice is dither. In computerese, dithering is the technique for mixing two or more colors together to create the illusion of extra colors and is used in computer systems that have limited color resolution. The third choice is to let Netscape substitute the next closest color. The best choice is to leave the default setting on automatic and let Netscape decide how to handle the colors. If the choice is too annoying, the settings can be changed for a given site but remember to change them back. Leave the While Loading box checked.

Next select Applications from the Preferences list. Applications may be referred to as Helper Applications (Fig. 17-3) because they help Netscape do things it cannot do by itself. After the Applications button, the Supporting Applications box appears. Four settings are listed: Telnet Application, TN3270, View Source, and Temporary Directory. In the Telnet Application blank type the location and name of the Telnet client selected for use with Netscape. For example if the program selected is QVT/Term then type c:\QVT/Term in the blank. If Windows 95

FIGURE 17-3. Some audiovisual files need helper applications to display or play the file.

is being used, simply type **telnet** in the blank. The second blank can be ignored. TN3270 is a special Telnet program for IBM 3270 machines. Few are still being used so the lack of a Telnet program for 3270 should not be a problem. The View Source directory is only needed if the user has a special program for viewing the source code, such as hypertext markup language, from a particular Web page. If the line is left blank, Netscape displays source code in its built-in window, which can be edited or saved. The Temporary Directory must be completed so Netscape knows were to put files that are being viewed. First a temporary file directory must be created on the hard drive. If Windows 3.1 is being used go to the File Manager and select **New**. Name the new directory temp or tmp if another temporary directory already exits. For Windows 95 doubleclick on the my computer icon. Then doubleclick on the disk drive in which the temporary directory or folder is to be placed. On the File menu, point to New, and then click Folder and type the name of the folder temp file.

The best reference on Netscape 2.0 is by R. Schwerin, entitled *How to Use Netscape Navigator 2.0,* published in 1996 by Ziff-Davis Press. It costs $25 and provides screen-by-screen instructions.

CHAPTER 18

▪▪▪▪▪▪▪▪▪▪▪▪▪▪▪▪▪▪▪▪▪▪▪▪▪▪▪▪▪▪▪▪▪▪▪▪

Search Tools

The Web has become extremely large. Finding anything useful requires the talents of a private investigator (PI). On the Web, PIs (Fig. 18-1) include directories, lists, archives, and search engines. Most search engines keep track of the Web a little better than the one in Figure 18-2.

There are five general types of search tools that are useful in locating information on the Web. An overview is provided in Display 18-1. The first type is a directory of information about Internet sites usually organized by subject or topics that can be searched by subject or keyword. How complete the directory is depends on the owner or developer. Some directories claim to list only the best sites (according to the owner's or developer's criteria). Others try to be more comprehensive. Subject directories are useful for beginners or for finding information about a new topic but may be limited in retrieval for more experienced users.

The next type of search tool is a specialized list of what is new or cool or unique. These lists also depend on the developer's criteria. Generally, lists of new Web pages are based on a specific time frame such as 3 days or a week. The list contains the names and uniform resource locators (URLs) of Web pages that came online within the past few days. Lists of what is cool or unique are usually referencing sites with some unusual feature related to the use of multimedia or type of content. Some may be enjoyable, whereas others may not be suitable for more sensitive viewers.

A third type of search tool is archived or stored data. These sites provide access to material at one single point instead of having to look at multiple sites to gather the information. Archival sites exist for software, newsgroup messages, and Gopher sites, for example.

A fourth search tool is search engines. Search engines look through a data base for the information requested on a search topic. The search engine data

Hunting for
something?
Try using a
search engine.

FIGURE 18-1. Search engines act as private investigators on the web.

base is created by a computer program that visits individual Web pages and retrieves selected data from each page such as the title, the URL, and first few lines of text. This information is added to the data base created by the search engine. Users sign on to the search engine and state the topic of interest. The data base is searched and a list of sites meeting the criteria is displayed on the monitor.

Finally, there are metasearch engines. Metasearch engines have selected several of the individual search tools and grouped them together on one or two Web pages. The search tools function the same as when they are accessed individually. Convenience is the primary reason for using a metasearch engine.

SELECTING A SEARCH STRATEGY

Most search tools are designed to permit the user to search a keyword or short phrase. The keyword should be a noun such as the name of a person, place, or thing. Use the singular form of a noun. Most search tools automatically search the root word by removing common plural endings and then adding the more common plural forms. A phrase composed of adjectives and nouns is also acceptable. Thus, the term **case management** can be searched. However, the term **case management** may not retrieve sources where the term **case manager** is used. When in doubt about what is being searched, try alternate forms. For example, try searching both the words splints and splinting.

Now, Where IS that track?

FIGURE 18-2. A lost engine searching for its track.

DISPLAY 18-1. SEARCH TOOLS ON THE INTERNET

Single Search Engines

Alta Vista	http://altavista.digital.com
Excite	http://www.excite.com
Hot Bot	http://www.hotbot.com
Infoseek Guide	http://guide.infoseek.com
Infoseek Ulta	http://ultra.infoseek.com
Inktomi	http://inktomi.berkeley.edu/query.html
Lycos	http://www.lycos.com
Open Text	http://www.opentext.com
NlightN	http://www.nlightn.com
WWW Worm	http://wwww.cs.colorado.edu/wwww
Web Crawler	http://www.webcrawler.com

Metasearch Engines

All4one	http://all4one/com
All-in-One Search	http://www.albany.net/allinone/
CUSI	http://www-eecs.nwu.edu/cusi.html
Highway 61	http://www.highway62.com/
IBM's Infomarket	http://www.infomkt.ibm.com
Inso	http://wizard.inso.com
Internet Slueth	http://www.sleuth.com
MetaCrawler	http://www.metacrawler.com
Metasearch	http://metasearch.com
Mother Load	http://www.cosmix.com/motherload/insane/
Netsearch	http://home.mcom.com/home/internet-search.html
ProFusion	http://www.designlab.ukans.edu/ProFusion.html
Savvysearch	http://guaraldi.cs.colostate.edu:2000/form
Search Engine Room	http://www.nosc.mil:80/plant_earth/Library/sei_room.html
SearchPlex	http://www.west.net/~jbc/tools/search.html
Snake Eyes	http://www.geocities.com/SiliconValley/6937/snakeiz.html
SuperSeek	http://w3.superseek.com/superseek
Starting Point Metasearch	http://www.stpt.com/search.html
Ted Slater's Search Engine Collection	http://www.regent.edu/~tedslat/tools.html
W3 Catalog	http://cuiwww.unige.ch/w3catalog/
W3 Search Engines	http://cuiwww.unige.ch/meta-index.html
Web Search	http://www.biddeford.com/~soaring/

Subject Directories

Apollo	http://apollo.co.uk
Clearinghouse	http://www.lib.umich.edu/chhome.html
Cyberhound	http://www.thomson.com/cyberhound/
Excite Netdirectory	http://www.excite.com/Subject/

(continued)

DISPLAY 18-1. SEARCH TOOLS ON THE INTERNET (CONTINUED)

Galaxy	http://galaxy.einet.net
Hoover's Online	http://hoovweb.hoovers.com/
Infomine	http://lib-www.ucr.edu/govinfo.html
Linkstar	http://www.linkstar.com
Magellan	http://www.mckinley.com
New Rider's Yellow Pages	http://www.mcp.com/newriders/wwwyp/
Nynex Yellow Pages	http://www.niyp.com
Pointcom	http://www.pointcom.com
Reuters Health Information	http://www.reutershealth.com/
Starting Point	http://www.stpt.com
Tribal Voice	http://www.tribal.com/search.htm
Whole Internet Catalog	http://nearnet.gnn.com/wic/
WWW Virtual Library	http://www.w3.org/hyper text/DataSources/bySubject/Overview.html
World Wide Yellow Pages	http://www.vyp.com
Yahoo	http://www.yahoo.com
The Yellow Pages	http://theyellowpages.com

What's New

NSCA What's New	http://www.csa.uiuc.edu/SDG/Software/Mosaic/Docs/whats-new.html
Net-Happenings	http://www.midline/NET/
Netscape What's New	http://www.netscape.com/escapes/what_new.html
New and/or Exciting	http://www.lsu.edu//poli/newexcit.html
Starting Point	http://www.stpt.com/new.html
What's New on Yahoo	http://www.yahoo.com/new/
What's New Too	http://newtoo.manifest.com

Internet Archives

Bigfoot	http://www.bigfoot.com
Fourll Directory	http://www.four11.com
Internet address finder	http://www.iaf.net
Lookup	http://www.lookup.com/lookup/search.html
Whowhere?	http://whowhere.com
Alex gopher to:	gopher.lib.nscu.edu (and select)/Library Without Walls/Electronic Journals
Archie telenet to:	archie/rutgers.edu **or to** archie.sura.net and log in as **archie**
Galaxy	http://galaxy.einet.net/gopher/gopher.html
Internic	gopher://ds.internic.net:4320/netfind
Veronica gopher to:	gopher.unr.edu and select/search
DejaNews	http://www.dejanews.com
Sift	http://sift.stanford.edu
Reference	http://www.reference.com

(continued)

DISPLAY 18-1. SEARCH TOOLS ON THE INTERNET (CONTINUED)

Computer/Software Collections

Clip Art Connection	http://www.acy.digex.net/~infomart/clipart/index.html
Intel	http://www.intel.com/
Macromedia!	http://www-1.macromedia.com/
Shareware	http://www.shareware.com
Silicon Surf	http://www.sgi.com/
Tucows	http://www.tucows.com

Reference Tools

Encyclopaedia Britannica	http://www.cb.com/
Library of Congress	http://www.loc.gov/
New York Public Library	http://gopher.nypl.org/
Research-It!	http://www.iTools.com/research-it/research-it.html
Switchboard	http://www.switchboard.com
Virtual Reference Desk	http://thorplus.lib.purdue.edu/reference/index.html

Not Operating at the Time of Survey

Jump Station II	Information indicates it has been discontinued
NIKOS	Information indicates it has been discontinued

Most search tools will not search or retrieve words that are verbs, adverbs, prepositions, or full sentences. Conjunctions should be used with care because several are used as representatives for mathematical formulas. Do not use the conjunctions *and, or, not, and not,* or *but not* except as specified in the search engine instructions. (See section on Applying the Search Strategy.) The following examples are not good search strategies:

1. Show me Web pages on splint making.
2. Find all splints used with arthritic patients.
3. Pediatric practice in physical therapy
4. Early intervention programs for multiply disabled children run by occupational therapists
5. Information on aphasia in stroke patients

Better approaches for the above questions are:

1. Splint
2. Splints and arthritis (see *Applying the Search Strategy* on p. 117)
3. Pediatric physical therapy
4. Early intervention and occupational therapy
5. Aphasia and stroke not volume (see *Applying the Search Strategy* on p. 117)

The first example should be tried first with only the main keyword. A follow-up search using the word splinting may be tried depending on the results of the first search.

The second search needs two keyword words. Also some search engines require that a plus sign (+) be used instead of the conjunction and. Thus, example 2 might be typed +splints +arthritis. Others allow the user to specify how many terms are to be matched. The word *match* is usually equivalent to the word *and* in search strategy development.

For the third search only the most important words are searched. If the words pediatric occupational therapy appear, the subject is likely to be about practice. Generally fewer search terms, not more, results in the best retrieval. The concept of fewer applies to search number 4 as well. Check to see how much information is available on early intervention before restricting the search. Also in issues related to education the user should remember that the term *related services* might include occupational therapy, physical therapy, or speech pathology even if professions are not named in the document.

The fifth search is phrased to reduce the number of unrelated Web pages returned with the search results. The term stroke can be used for a disease or a measure of blood flow (stroke volume) and appears within the word keystroke. Thus a better search is designed by having the search engine remove documents that talk about stroke volume. Some search engines require that the search be stated using the minus sign (−). The search, therefore, would read stroke −volume. Any attempt to eliminate a term from the search retrieval must be carefully reviewed so that good retrieval is not lost by removing an unwanted term. For example, the search strategy occupational therapy not physical therapy is not a good approach. Removing the word therapy from one side of the search strategy also removes it from the other. Therefore, no Web page with the word therapy in it will be displayed. Changing the search to read occupational therapy not physical is an improvement but not much because both subjects frequently appear. The best approach is to emphasize occupational therapy and not worry if the term physical therapy also appears. Thus, the best strategy is +occupational +therapy or tell the search engine to match both terms.

BEST SEARCH ENGINES

The best search engine is the one that finds the information of interest to the user. Some search engines, however, are easier to control than others. One of the easier is HotBot (Fig. 18-3). In the box after **Search for**: type the word, words, or word phrase to be searched. Then select from the next box to the right the phrase which best describes how the search should be performed. The choices are: All the words, Any of the words, The exact phrase, The person, Links to this URL, or The Boolean expression. Then select the number of results to be retrieved from the choices: 10, 15, 50, 75, or 100. Finally, click on the **Search** button. Other op-

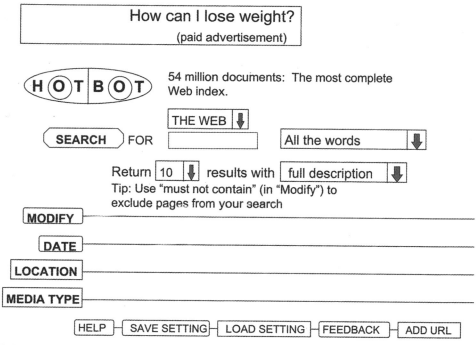

FIGURE 18-3. HotBot search template.

tions are available, as shown in Figure 18-4, that allow the searcher to futher modify the search by date, location, and type of media to be retrieved.

Other good search engines are AltaVista, Inktomi, and Infoseek. One problem with Infoseek is that printing is not permitted. To print from an Infoseek search it is necessary to select a metasearch engine that includes Infoseek such as Metasearch. Webcrawler used to be a favorite search engine and is still mentioned in many texts about the Internet. However, the search engine is not being updated so it is of limited value. The search engine, Excite, searches well but does not print out the URLs, which means if the user does not have time to view all the sites retrieved in the search, the search will have to be repeated because the URLs are not printed to allow them to be entered directly.

APPLYING THE SEARCH STRATEGY

An example may clarify why understanding how to control the search is so important. Most search engines do not warn the user that the default mathematical formula is "or." This means that if the user is looking for the phrase **case management**, the search engine will look for the word case **OR** the word management **OR** both. Although some of the sites returned by search engine will have both, many will have only the word case, whereas others have the word manage-

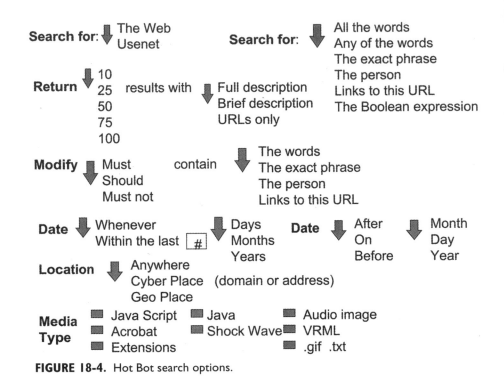

FIGURE 18-4. Hot Bot search options.

ment. In other words, the search engine may find the phrase "case of beer" or "management of a baseball team." Neither has much to do with the concept of case management. To avoid the problem, the user should type *case* AND *management*. Some search engines prefer the phrase to be typed as *case +management* and occasionally in quotation marks, "case management." The options illustrate the importance of reading the instructions about entering search terms and boolean logic. Boolean logic is named for George Boole, a mathematician, who first wrote about the mathematical formulas used to search most data bases. The common operators are "and," "or," and "not." The formula "and" requires **all** terms in the search request to appear in the document or record. The formula "or" allows **any one** of the search terms or all of the terms to be present. The formula for "not" **excludes** any document in which the search term(s) appear. Generally it is a good idea not to use "not" unless the user is sure of its action.

Usually the best terms are nouns or adjective-noun combinations. Never type a sentence. Avoid verbs, adverbs, and prepositions. For example, to search for activities of daily living, the search should be entered as *activities and daily and living*. To include the acronym, type *activities and daily and living or adl*. If the user is unsure how the search engine will search and the instructions are vague, the best strategy is to try combinations. For example, the search for activities of daily living could be entered as *activities and daily and living, activities +daily +living,* "activities daily living," or on Hot Bot choose the option "Exact phrase."

CHAPTER 19

■■■■■■■■■■■■■■■■■■■■■■■■■■■■■■■■■■

Those Darn Error Messages

There's this nifty new Web site to try out. According to Cousin Jim the uniform resource locator (URL) is http://this.is.gonna.be/fun_city. When you type in the URL, you get one of those disgusting error messages. What do they mean? What do you do next? Here are some of the more common error messages and the solutions, sometimes.

UNABLE TO LOCATE HOST

This error message means that either the URL was mistyped or it is temporarily out of service. Carefully check the typed address to be sure it is correct. If the typing is correct the computer may be out of service. Out of service can indicate that a computer crashed, is busy updating or removing files, or has been set to ignore incoming requests via the Internet so the computer space can be used for local tasks such as compiling numerous files to write a large grant request.

NOT FOUND

The requested object does not exist on this server. The link you followed is either outdated or inaccurate, or the server has been instructed not to let you have it. Please inform the site administrator of the *referring page*.

This error message occurs when the user follows a link that no longer is in service. The message asks the user to notify the Webmaster of the page on which the link was found that the link no longer exists. To do so, use the Back button to return to source of the link. If the link is a homepage, the Webmaster's name and E-mail address should appear at the bottom of the page. If the page is not a homepage, check at the bottom or top of the page for a button that takes the user to the homepage. If no button is available, click on the URL and remove all file names to the right of the first forward slash and press Enter. The remaining URL should go to the homepage or provide information on accessing the homepage.

404 NOT FOUND

The requested URL this.is.gonna.be/fun_city was not found on this server.
Check to be sure the typing is correct. Computers are fussier than an English teacher about correct order of letters and numbers. Check to make sure all the letters and numbers are present. Check the 0 (zero) and letter O. Check the 1 (one) and letter l. If none of those common problems are the culprit, try leaving off all the file names after the forward slash and type only the host address. If the host address connects, the file names may have changed. Looking at the homepage may provide direction to the right file and its new name. A message may be sent to the Webmaster listed at the bottom of the homepage requesting assistance in locating the file. If the host address does not connect, either the host name is wrong, the server is temporarily down, or the server is permanently decommissioned. Try using one of search engines to see if another host has a copy of fun_city file. Another host may be a mirror site for the one that is out of commission.

ERROR

Requested document (URL this.is.gonna.be/fun_city) could not be accessed.
This message means the document exists in the computer's directory files but for some reason the host computer is not able to display the document or is unable to access it. The host computer may be malfunctioning, the file may be damaged, or special permission may be required to view the file. Go to the homepage (delete the file names after the forward slash) and click on the Webmaster's name. Write the Webmaster an E-mail asking if there is a problem. If permission is needed, request information about the qualifications. If the answer is permission denied, use a search engine to see if the file exists elsewhere and does not require special permission.

APPLICATION NOT FOUND

The helper file (application) is not available or the browser does not know where to find it. Check to see what application is needed. For example, if the URL is to a data base such as a library catalog, the helper file is a Telnet client (software program). Netscape does not have a built-in Telnet client. A Telnet client must be obtained (see Chapter 13 for Telnet names and locations), loaded on the computer, and Netscape instructed in the Applications menu where (path and file name) to find the Telnet client (Fig. 19-1).

FIGURE 19-1. There is a better solution. Get a copy of a Telnet client, install it, and tell Netscape where to find it.

HELPER APPLICATION NOT FOUND

This is similar to the above message. Netscape cannot locate the needed helper application. It occurs most frequently when the user is trying to download a file. Check the extension on the file to be downloaded and then check the list of available helpers under Options, go to Preferences, select Applications, and look at the list of helpers. Click on one if it can handle the file extension of the file to be downloaded. A list of file extensions is provided in Chapter 12.

403 FORBIDDEN

The user does not have permission to visit that Web site. There are three choices: Try to contact the Webmaster and ask for permission. Use a search engine to locate a Web site with the same or similar file where permission is not required. Forget it. There are lots of other fish in the sea.

CONNECTION REFUSED BY HOST

This message is not the same as 403 Forbidden. Usually this message means the computer is temporarily not accepting connections but the URL does exit. The computer may be down for maintenance. Try later.

FILE CONTAINS NO DATA

The URL is addressing a file that contains nothing or a Web page that appears to be blank. Sometimes that error can be corrected by adding the port number *:80* to the end of the host name but before the file name extensions. Example: this.is.gonna.be:80/fun_city.

TOO MANY USERS ARE CONNECTED TO THIS SERVER

The site is very popular and too many users are trying to access too few ports on the host computer. Try again at a nonpeak time such as late at night or early in the morning. For night owls, 3 AM is a good time.

BAD FILE REQUEST

This message occurs when the form of the URL is incorrect. Putting commas instead of periods is one incorrect form. Another is typing three parts of the URL instead of four, or typing five parts instead of four. Example: this.is.gonnabe/. Note there are only three parts and two periods when there should be four parts and three periods. Occasionally the problem is erroneous hypertext markup language coding on the Webmaster's part. This occurs when the Web site is new. If the Webmaster's E-mail is known, send a message suggesting a coding error may be the problem.

TCP ERROR ENCOUNTERED WHILE SENDING REQUEST TO SERVER

This (transmission control protocol) is a network problem. Data were not sent correctly. Try again. If the message occurs more than three times, contact the systems administrator and tell him or her the exact wording of the message.

FAILED DNS LOOKUP

The domain name server (DNS) is not working to convert the URL to the correct Internet protocol (IP) address. A quick solution is to try typing the numeric IP address, if known. Otherwise double check the spelling or wait a while for the DNS computer to be put back online.

NNTP SERVER ERROR

Be sure the name of the network news transfer protocol (NNTP) host is entered correctly under Options, Preferences, Mail, and News. If this information is correct the host may be too busy. Try again later.

CANNOT ADD FORM SUBMISSION RESULT TO BOOKMARK LIST

Bookmark URLs or IP addresses must be from the original site. A link from a search engine, for example, cannot be used because it is not the original site. In the coded language the extension "cgi-bin" is always a sign that the URL is not from the original site.

CHAPTER 20

■■

Graphics, Video, and Sound on the Web

OVERVIEW

Many graphic and audiovisual items on the Web are byte and speed hogs, meaning they take many memory bytes to create and a great deal of speed to view or hear. For example, to view video in real time, that is, the speed at which it was recorded, the modem connection is important, especially the bandwidth. Video data take up enormous space. For example, suppose a picture frame of 160 × 120 pixels (individual dots on the screen) is being transferred. Each frame would use 9,600 bytes of memory before it is compressed. Each second of live video requires 15 frames or more. In other words 14,400 bytes of information per second is required to display a small black and white image. The example is for video only, with no audio included.

Compression is the best method of transmitting data. The compression ratio may be up to 20:1, which decreases the bits per second (bps) to 7,200 bps. When audio is added the video can just barely be received on a 14,400 bps. For some large graphics, the speed will need to be at 28,800 bps.

GRAPHICS

Many types of graphics are available on the Internet (Fig. 20-1). There are famous paintings, totally unknowns' paintings, good photographs, bad photographs, useful clip art, useless clip art, beautiful designs, ugly designs, publicity shots of the famous and the infamous, weather maps for yesterday and tomorrow, pictures of movie and television stars, business logos, cartoons, animations, drawings, watercolors, charcoals, pastels, oil paint, colored pencils, movies, video clips, images of the human body, and more. On Web pages, graph-

FIGURE 20-1. Graphics take many memory bytes to create and a great deal of speed to view.

ics may be inline graphics, which are part of the Web page itself. Inline graphics include bullet points, decorations, illustrations, logos, and separators. Other graphics are separate image files that can be downloaded to a hard drive for later viewing. Separate image files also require helper applications to be viewed. Table 20-1 shows the graphic display helpers. The most frequently used is LView or LView Pro. Viewers can be downloaded from http://www.tucows.com, a large site for shareware software programs or ftp://ftp.ncsa.uiuc.edu/Mosaic/Windows/viewers. Table 20-2 contains common file extensions and their meanings.

Graphics, however, require more than the minimum equipment. The central processing unit should be at least a 486SX running at 25 MHz with an acceler-

TABLE 20-1. TYPES OF IMAGE FILES AND HELPER APPLICATIONS REQUIRED		
Type of Files	**File Name Extensions**	**Helper Application Needed**
Graphics and Photos	JPG, JPEG, GIF, BMP, PCX	LView, LView Pro, or PaintShop Pro
	TIF, TIFF	Lview Pro
Audio and Sounds	AU, AIF, SBI	Netscape Audio Player, WHAM!, or Wplany
	MIDI	Windows Media Player
	WAV	Windows Sound Recorder or WHAM!
Videos	MPG, MPEG	MPEGPlay or WMPEG
	MOV	QuickTime
Audiovisuals	AVI	Video for Windows or Avi Pro

TABLE 20-2. AUDIO AND VISUAL FILE NAME EXTENSIONS AND FULL NAMES	
Extension	**Name**
.bmp	BMP, Bitmap Windows Graphic Image
.gif	GIF, CompuServe Graphics Interchange Format
.jpeg, .jpg, .jfif	JPEG, JFIF (Joint Photographic Experts Group File Interchange Format)
.midi	MIDI, Musical Instrument Digital Interface
.mpg, .mpeg	MPEG, Motion Picture Experts Group
.tiff, .tif	TIFF, Tagged Image File Format

ated graphics card. The graphics card is most important for the quality of the image. It should be built into the system's motherboard or should be connected through a VESA local bus (VL-bus) or peripheral component interconnect (PCI) expansion slot. Older video cards may work but the quality will be poor. Older cards can only display 256 colors, whereas newer graphic cards can display over a million.

AUDIO

Audio files on the Internet have been increasing rapidly with the advent of audio software programs (Fig. 20-2).

The four major audio programs are listed in Table 20-3. RealAudio is the best known. About 350 sites offer RealAudio files. The best site is AudioNet at http://www.audionet.com, which has the largest variety of RealAudio files. RealAudio software must be directed to a RealAudio server.

Audio files using Xing Streamworks are listed at http://www.xingtech.com/content/sw1_content.html.

The newest development is radio on the Internet. WOR-AM in New York City went online early this year. The sound is not perfect. Audio software pro-

FIGURE 20-2. Music and sound can be found in audio files.

TABLE 20-3. AUDIO PROGRAMS		
Program	**Location**	**Comment**
RealAudio 1.0 for 14,400	http://www.realaudio.com	Progressive Network
RealAudio 2.0 for 28,800	http://www.realaudio.com	Comes with Windows95
Streamworks	http://www.xingtech.com	Xing Technology
Internet Wave	http://www.vocaltec.com	VocalTec
TrueSpeech	http://www.dspg.com	DSP Group

grams have a way to go to achieve quality sound, but the speech is understandable. A list of stations is available at http://www.radiotv.com/realaudio.htm. News is available at http://www.cnet.com/Radio.

NetRadio at http://www.netradio.net is another concept. NetRadio offers its own programming designed to provide background music while the user surfs the Internet for other items of interest.

RealAudio has also been used to promote new records. At the Web site http://www.atlantic-records.com the user can listen to audio clips of new albums.

Another site offering various online music stores is http://www.interjuke.com. The site at http://wso.william.edu/~mgarland/sounds/ provides files of television theme songs. For movie themes try http://www.moviesounds.com.

MOVIE CLIPS

Movie clips are usually stored in three formats: QuickTime, Motion Picture Experts Group (MPEG), or Video for Windows (Fig. 20-3). Netscape does not provide viewers for QuickTime or MPEG so they must be downloaded. The Quick-Time viewer can be downloaded from http://www.tucows.com. Tucows is a large site for shareware programs with many mirror sites (copies). Click on your state or country of residence for the site closest to you. Locate the QuickTime

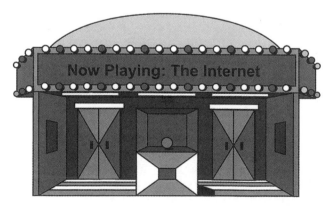

FIGURE 20-3. Movies and movie clips.

viewer and download from that site to avoid delays in service. Use PkUnzip or WinZip to uncompress the file. Copies of compression programs are also available from Tucows.

MPEG is available from the same site. Its extension will be mpegw32.zip or similar. It will also need to be uncompressed.

Microsoft Video is available in Windows. To find it go to the Control Panel and select Drivers. If it does not show up, it can be downloaded from ftp.microsoft.com in the /developer/dr/Multimedia directory. Look for a file name such as wv1160.exe or later.

Some interesting sites to visit are:

http://www.yahoo.com/Computers/Multimedia/

http://www.cnam.fr/ (French)

http://deathstar.rutgers.edu/people/bochkay/movies.html

Shockwave is a plug-in program available for Netscape that allows users to view the <EMBED> tag in the hyptertext markup language (HTML) documents. Shockwave lets you view Macromedia Director movies, games, and audio files. For information see Shockwave's homepage at **http://www.macromedia.com**. To download Shockwave type the following uniform resource locator (URL): **http://www.macromedia.com/shockwave/download**. Look for the correct file for the Netscape program (Mac, Windows 3.1, or Windows 95) and download that program. The same site provides examples of how Shockwave can be used.

VIRTUAL REALITY

What is referred to as virtual reality (VR) or virtual worlds on the Internet are three-dimensional pages constructed using virtual reality modeling language (VRML). To enter a virtual world requires either a VR Web browser or a plug-in program installed in the Web browser. The plug-in program for Netscape is WebFX by PaperSoftware. To retrieve WebFX go to Netscape's homepage, **http://home.netscape.com**/ for any messages regarding WebFX. Then type in PaperSoftware's homepage, **http://www.paperinc.com**/. Follow the instructions for downloading. If a \temp (temporary) directory has been made, download the WebTX file to the \temp directory. If a \temp directory has not been made, create one by going to the DOS prompt such as c:> and type **mkdir \temp**. Then go back to the PaperSoftware homepage and download the file.

WebFX will decompress automatically. Use the Setup program to install it. Click the Next button after installation is complete, which will display the Netscape program Directory dialogue box. Confirm the Destination Directory is correct such as c:\Netacape2\Program. Continue to follow the instructions. The program should complete installation without a problem but checking is always a good idea. To start the program after installation, click on the WebFX icon, which will start both WebFX and Netscape. The screen should show a big N on the left and a list of options. What's Cool will provide some three-dimensional demonstrations.

Using the mouse for three-dimensional sites will take some practice. The user can move in any direction including up, down, below, through, and so forth. If confused, lost, or disoriented, he or she may click the reset button at the bottom of the page. It returns the original display so that the user can start again or exit.

VIDEOCONFERENCING

Videoconferencing allows two people or a group of people to communicate by means of typed text, audio and video across a computer network, or on the worldwide Internet. Each person can be a sender, a receiver, or both (Fig. 20-4).

The major videoconferencing system is called CU-SeeMe, pronounced "See you, See me." It was developed at Cornell University, thus the CU is both a play on letters and the initials of the university where the work was done. The CU-SeeMe programming language is compatible with the Internet protocol. Macintosh and Windows clients are available.

Equipment for videoconferencing includes a video monitor capable of providing 16 levels of gray or color. Most color monitors can display 256 colors or better so the monitor is rarely a problem. Each user must be connected to the Internet using Internet protocol. To transmit video, the user must have a video camera and a digitizer board. Some multimedia Macintoshes have a video digitizer built into the computer. Most Windows users will need to buy one. A camera/digitizer package is available for both Macintosh and Windows computers in a combined package that looks like a golf ball with a miniature camera lens built into it. It costs about $100 and is available at most computer stores. The trade name is Connectix QuickCam.

FIGURE 20-4. Video conferencing.

Video resolution is available in two levels: high-quality 320 × 240 pixels or low-quality 160 × 120 pixels. A pixel is a single dot on a monitor or in a bitmapped image. As the number of pixels increases, the image begins to look more like a photograph instead of a collection of dots. At present the high-quality video is available only for Macintosh-to-Macintosh connections. The Windows version supports only low-resolution video. The quality of the audio depends on a combination of factors such as the computer processing speed, the speakers, microphone, and the audio board, which should be capable of handling full duplex. Most sound boards handle half duplex, which means the transmission can occur in only one direction at a time. Macintosh machines usually have full duplex but Windows machines may or may not, depending on the type of sound board installed.

The speed of the connection is important in determining the amount of sound and video data that can be sent and received. Faster connections (eg, greater bandwidth) produce better quality. A 14.4-Kbps modem will not process the 16K per second of information to be sent or received. A 18.8-Kbps modem is just barely fast enough to carry the audio but not the video. Integrated service digital networks can handle both the audio and video. Fiberoptic cable is better. CU-SeeMe was not designed for low-bandwidth (modem) connections. Nevertheless, slower speeds do not make videoconferencing impossible, just not as smooth in motion or as clear as pure tones. The video will jump because the frames per second are not refreshed fast enough to fool the human eye into reporting the movement as continuous. Old movies had that problem. They made movement seem jerky. The sound may lack a few bass tones and break up but it can be recognized. Some people find that typing messages on slower connections is easier to accept than sounds that mimic an old phonograph record.

The best part of CU-SeeMe is that it is available free from Cornell University at http://cu-seeme.cornell.edu or ftp://cu-seeme.cornell.edu/pub/cu-seeme. There is a README.First file that should be read to find out the latest information about CU-SeeMe. Macintosh users should look for files that start with Mac.CU-SeeMe followed by a number-letter combination. Get the highest number available because that will be the latest version. Windows users should look for a file that starts with Pc.CU-SeeMe followed by a number-letter combination. Again the highest number indicates the latest version. There is also a CU-SeeMe.FAQ file that should answer some commonly asked questions. For other videoconferencing programs see Table 20-4.

Some suggestions for running a videoconference can make for a better event. First, a videoconference should be interactive. To facilitate interaction the equipment needs to be set up to allow point and click change from presenter to each person in the audience at each site. Pressure-sensitive panels are available and can be programmed to provide point and click ease.

Second, lecturers need to be trained to use the videoconferencing technology to its best advantage. Each lecturer should practice using the equipment before actually presenting. Practice should include sitting in the audience to get the view of the audience as well as presenting. Practice as a presenter should include changing the view from the presenter's face, viewing a paper under the docu-

TABLE 20-4. VIDEOCONFERENCING PROGRAMS AVAILABLE ON THE INTERNET

Program Name	Location	Type
CinoVideo/Direct	http://www.cinecom.com/CineCom/cinvdrct.html	Shareware
Enhanced CU-SeeMe 16 bit or 32 bit	http://goliath.wpine.com/cu-seeme.html	Shareware
FreeVue	http://www.freevue.com	Shareware
VidCall	http://www.access.digex.net/~vidcall/vidcall.html	Commercial
EMULive	http://www.jcs-canada.com/emulive.html	Shareware
VDOPhone	http://www.vdolive.com/vdophone/	Shareware

ment viewer, and viewing the audience. The lecturer should also practice shifting from speaking to explaining or showing a document to using another audiovisual item such as slides. Smooth transition is important to help the audience focus on the presentation and not on whether the equipment is going to be manipulated smoothly or awkwardly. The lecturer should also check to see how well the camera views different audiovisual media such as photographs, charts, figures, slides, videotapes, and computer software programs. Handouts should be sent to remote sights before the lecture is given. Faxing is acceptable for text but the font should be easy to read. Fonts with serifs do not always fax well. Although photographs, figures, and tables can be faxed, unless the receiving fax is of high quality, sending copies through the mail service or via the Internet may provide more satisfactory copies. If small items are to be shown and used during the presentation, duplicate sets sent to the remote sites may provide a better learning opportunity.

Third, the conference room should be carefully planned with videoconferencing as its major purpose. Lighting is important. There should be enough light to illuminate the lecture area and the audience. However, the light should not cause glare in the camera view. Sound must be loud enough to be hear over distances but not so loud as to cause annoying feedback. Sound pickup must be sensitive enough so the amplification begins immediately when any speaker talks whether the speaker is a lecturer or an audience participant. The room should be arranged so the camera can see all members of the audience. Chairs arranged on tiers is actually better than a flat room if a large audience must be accommodated. Monitors should be placed so the lecturer and the audience can see each other clearly. Two monitors are essential—one for the lecturer to view the audience and the second for the audience to view the lecturer. Temperature should also be controlled. Extremes in temperature can change the visual and sound projection.

Usually, a videoconferencing room will need at least two cameras; three would be better. One should be used for the lecturer, one for the audience, and one for the documents. The camera for the lecturer should be set for fixed clear viewing of the face and upper body. The audience camera will need to be set for fixed viewing at a distance consistent with the size of the room. The document camera needs to be able to zoom in and out so the lenses must have greater magnification than required for the other two cameras. A document camera provides much better viewing than using an overhead projector. The document camera can also be used for viewing three-dimensional objects.

If all this discussion about equipment and space is overwhelming, there is another way to use teleconferencing without the fuss and finances: call Kinko's. Yes, that's the copy company. Kinko's is putting in teleconferencing centers in many larger cities. The Internet address is http://www.fortnet.org/Kinkos/video. Of course, there will be a charge, but the experience may well be worth the cost. They can provide guidance and knowledge until the user has gained some first-hand experience.

CHAPTER 21

■■■■■■■■■■■■■■■■■■■■■■■■■■■■■■■■■■■■■■■

Building a Homepage With HTML

Hypertext markup language (HTML) is in its third version. It consists of tags that tell other software what to do. Most tags are placed in on-off pairs that control the structure of the page or document. The tag with a forward slash is the off command; the tag with no slash is the on command. Each tag starts and ends with the less than and greater than signs called wickets (<>). Tags are not case sensitive. Some major tags are discussed in the following section.

<HTML> </HTML>

These two tags should be used to start and end an HTML page or document. Not all browsers depend on these tags to identify HTML documents, but it is a good habit to include them. As more languages are used to create pages on the Web, identifying the language quickly may speed up the process.

<HEAD> </HEAD>

The header does not display on the page. Its primary purpose is to identify the title tags.

<TITLE> </TITLE>

These tags identify the official title of the page. It is this title that is saved when a Web site is added to a bookmark in a browser such as Netscape Navigator. A good title should accurately describe the content of the page. Because many spiders and robots use the title as part of the information searched by search engines, an accurate title increases the chances of the page being identified in a search. A major purpose in creating a Web page is to attract attention to it. Properly representing it makes the Web page easier to locate and use.

<BODY> </BODY>

The body contains the important part of the Web page. Actually the term Web page can be misleading. Web pages can be many printed pages long. The body of a Web page could be an entire book.

<H1> </H1> THROUGH <H6> </H6>

Six sizes of fonts are used on Web pages. H1 is the largest and is usually reserved for major headings. H6 is the smallest and is used for long running text. H2 through H5 can be used for subheadings or to identify important points that need to stand out visually.

<STRONG> </STRONG>

The strong tag is another way of telling the Web browser that the information contained between the tags is important. Most browsers read the strong tags as a command to bold the text. Some browsers can also be directed to display strong tags in all capital letters or in a specific color such as red.

<A> </A>

This is the anchor code and is used to define a section of text as a hyperlink.

<B> </B>

If the Web construction master wants to make sure the text is read by the browser as bold, then these tags should be used.

<EM> </EM>

The emphasis tags are used when a specific word or phrase is to be emphasized so it stands out from the rest. Emphasis tags are usually read by browsers as italic text. Some browsers can be changed to display the emphasis tags as bold letters.

<I> </I>

To be sure that a text is displayed in italics, use these tags.

<ADDRESS> </ADDRESS>

The address tag gives identifying information about the Web page developer or Webmaster who is responsible for the content of the Web page. Usually the person's name, affiliation, and E-mail address are provided. Most Web browsers display the address in italics.

<LI> </LI>

The list tag is used to display items in text as an ordered or unordered list.

<OL> </OL>

The ordered list tag is used to indicate items are to be ordered with sequential numbers.

<UL> </UL>

The unordered list tag is used to indicate items are to be bulleted but not in a particular order.

The following commands are used singly, not in pairs.

<P>

The paragraph tag is used to designate the end of a paragraph. Without the paragraph tag the text will continue to wrap around. It is usually placed after the last word in a paragraph.

The break tag creates a blank line just as pressing the Enter key on the keyboard does. Break tags create spaces between various kinds of text and between text and graphics.

Display 21-1. SAMPLE WEB PAGE

```
<HTML>
<Head>
<Title>The Rehabilitation Team</Title>
</Head>
<Body>
<H1>The Members of the Rehabilitation Team</H1>
<H3>The rehabilitation team may be composed of many different specialists. They include
physicians, rehabilitation nurses, physical therapists, occupational therapists, speech lan-
guage pathologists, prosthetists, orthotists, therapeutic recreation specialists, kinesiothera-
pists, art therapists, dance therapists, music therapists, horticultural therapists, dietitians,
vocational rehabilitation counselors, medical social workers, special education teachers;
plus assistant level personnel such as licensed or practical nurses, physical therapy assis-
tants, and certified occupational therapy assistants.<P>
<A HREF="http://www.apta.org">American Physical Therapy Association.</Al>
<A HREF="http://www.yahoo.com">Yahoo</A>
<HR>
<ADDRESS>
The Rehabilitation Network<BR>
Everywhere USA<BR>
www.rehab.net.org<BR>
</ADDRESS>
</BODY>
</HTML>
```

<HR>

The horizontal tag draws a line. It is used to divide text or graphics from each other. The tag can be repeated if two lines are needed.

<IMG SRC = "FOO.GIF">

This tag indicates that a graphic image is to be inserted. The name after the equal sign is the actual name of the graphic. The .gif extension indicates the file is a graphic. Dozens of graphics are available on the Internet and on Web develop-ment CDs. SRC means source or source code.

Display 21-1 shows a sample Web page about rehabilitation team members.

SOME TIPS ON CREATING A GOOD WEB PAGE

1. Watch the color contrast between the background and foreground. May Web developers have gone overboard on the wallpaper back-

ground. It is either too busy, dizzy, or the wrong color to permit the text to be read and the graphics displayed. Good backgrounds stay in the background. They do not fight the foreground for visual dominance. Train the background to stay where it belongs, in back. In general, light shades of color with undefined or small patterns work best.

2. Watch the overall composition of the page. Use good design techniques. Good composition limits the number of objects (text and graphics) that are on one page so the eye and brain can follow the logic easily. Busy, dizzy pages tend to turn the reader off, confuse the reader, or both. The purpose of a Web page is communication. If a Web page developer wants to confuse the reader, clutter up the page. If clarity is important, keep the page organized around no more than three major text and graphic combinations.

3. Watch the spacing. Spacing is especially important if the Web page includes a form that the user is to complete. Allow enough space to complete the information without having to use shorthand. Spacing is also important to visual composition of the page. A few well placed blank spaces can greatly improve the visual attractiveness of the page.

4. Watch the size of the graphic. New Web page developers are often impressed with the graphic images available and decide to pick up a big one to impress everyone. Big graphic files are also big byte files. Big byte files take longer to load. Users get tired of waiting for a large file to load. They click the stop button and go on to another page that will load faster. Waiting for Web pages to load is like waiting in line at the ticket window or grocery store. Hardly anyone likes it!

5. White letters on a dark background is a tempting contrast. It is also a good approach if the purpose is to keep people from printing the information because white letters do not contrast well on white paper, which is usually the color in the print tray.

6. Use fonts that are easy to read. Some fonts are hard to read (Fig. 21-1).

Many HTML authoring tools are on the market, with prices ranging from free to $200. Directions and instructions are available for each. A summary of a few tools is provided in Table 21-1.

𝕬𝖛𝖔𝖎𝖉 𝖀𝖘𝖎𝖓𝖌 𝕱𝖆𝖓𝖈𝖞 𝕱𝖔𝖓𝖙𝖘 𝕿𝖍𝖆𝖙 𝕬𝖗𝖊 𝕯𝖎𝖋𝖋𝖎𝖈𝖚𝖑𝖙 𝕿𝖔 𝕽𝖊𝖆𝖉.

Avoid Using Fancy Fonts That Are Difficult To Read.

FIGURE 21-1. Some fonts are hard to read.

TABLE 21-1. HTML AUTHORING TOOLS

Name	Developer	Web Site	Free or Shareware
HotDog	Sausage Software	www.sausage.com	Shareware
HotDog Pro	Sausage Software	www.sausage.com	$49–69
HTML Assistant	Brooklyn North Software Works	ftp.cs.dal.ca/html/asst/	Freeware
Internet Assistant	Microsoft	www.microsoft.com/ msoffice/freestuf/msword/ download/ia/default.htm	Freeware
Web Author	Quarterdeck	www.qdeck.com/qdeck/ products/webAuthr/	$49.95
HTMLed	Peter Crawshaw	princgle.mta.ca/ pub/HTMLed	Shareware $39
PageMill 1.0	Adobe Inc.	www.adobe.com	$99
Spider 1.1	InContext Systems	www.incontext.com	$99
HoTMetaL Pro 2.0	SoftQuad	www.sq/com	$195
Web Wizard	ARTA Software	www.halcyon.com/web wizard/	

UNIT IV

USING THE INTERNET

CHAPTER 22

■■■■■■■■■■■■■■■■■■■■■■■■■■■■■■■■■■

Doing Research on the Internet

The Internet is a useful tool for gathering information to use in a formal or informal research project. Although the information is vast, the researcher must be able to state the problem clearly, analyze the type of information needed, and understand how the Internet is organized. Many textbooks on research methods outline the procedure for stating the problem. Therefore, this chapter concentrates on analyzing the information needed and locating it on the Internet.

Research needs vary with the research project. Needs may be to locate factual information such as names, dates, bibliographies, and products; opinions such as what is the best movie of the season; comparisons and contrasts such as rating the qualities of good software games; literature sources such as books and journals; and original source material such as the image of a famous painting, commentaries about famous writers, or conversations with experts.

Factual information is often available in reference works such as dictionaries, directories, almanacs, encyclopedias, and handbooks. Some useful sites are:

The Virtual Reference Desk http://thorplus.lib.purdue.edu/reference/index. html

Encyclopedia Britannica http://www.eb.com/

Grammar and style http://www.english.upenn.edu/~jlynch/grammar. html

Opinions are often expressed on newsgroups. Most topics about which a person might want an opinion are available by exploring the subjects covered by newsgroups. Of course, some Gopher and Web pages also contain opinions of the developer. DejaNews Research Service is an excellent search engine to locate newsgroup archives on many different subjects. The uniform resource locator is http://www.dejanews.com/.

Compare and contrast items, which rate the relative merits of products or subjects, are most often found on Gopher and Web pages. Archie documents may also provide evaluations.

Numerous good library catalogs are available on Gopher and Web. Some are:

Library of Congress http://www.loc.gov/

National Library of Medicine http://www.nlm.nih.gov/

New York Public Library http://gopher.nypl.org/

Houston Academy of Medicine-Texas Medical Center Library http://www. library.tmc.edu (links to numerous medical sites and electronic journals)

WebWise Library http://www.walcoff.com/library.index.html (links to newspapers, magazines, online books, and audiovisuals)

The MEDLINE data base is available at Healthgate http://www.healthgate. com/ and Physician Online at http://www.physicianonline.com/. Limited searching is available free. MEDLINE can also be searched by telneting directly to the data base. The software program Grateful Med is available from the National Technical Information Services for $29.95. Grateful Med is a menu-driven program in which the search strategy is developed offline. The online time is used only to connect to the data base, perform the search, and get offline. A typical search costs about $3. Remember to read the instructions for searching the data base for best results. The software program often determines the results.

Many types of information appear on the Internet. The researcher needs to know the general categories. Directory-type search engines are useful in learning the general and specific categories. Yahoo is one of the best at http://www. yahoo.com/. So are the print directories that are published every year.

Increasing numbers of journals and newsletters are being published in electronic form. Some have print counterparts and some are electronic only. Electronic publication, however, has several variations on the theme, especially if there is a print counterpart. Some journal publishers put only the table of contents online. The titles and authors of the articles appear but not the full text of the articles themselves. Other publishers put the abstracts online. The full abstract including title and authors is available but the full text of the article is not available. Still other publishers provide the full text of selected articles from an issue but not the full text of all articles. Some electronic journals provide the full text of all articles but not the news items, editorials, or letters to the editor. Finally there are complete, full text journal issues online. Most full text journals, however, require the reader to have a paid subscription to the print copy or to pay a fee to view the journal online. Publishers want their money. They do not intend to provide free subscriptions in any form. A few may provide full text to back issues after the issue has been published several months previously but that is about the best they will do. Even journals published only in electronic form require a subscription to view the full text. Do not expect to use the Internet as a cheap way to get access to journal literature. In the publishing world profit comes before altruism or scholarship.

There is one possible exception to the "no free access" to journal literature in electronic form. Some publishers permit libraries to provide free access to journals to which the library has a subscription. The idea is that a library user has access in the library to the journals so why not provide access via the library over the Internet. This means at many colleges and universities access to the electronic form of journals held by the library is available, usually through the library's homepage. However, access depends on the Internet protocol (IP) address and is restricted to campus host computers. In other words, at-home access will be denied unless the user is dialing into a campus computer and then selecting the library. The IP address provided by the Internet service provider will not be on the approved list of IPs for electronic journal access; only the IP address of an on-campus computer will be approved. To remove the on-campus restriction some libraries will require the user to type in a valid library card number. No valid library card number, no access!

Although only a few full textbooks are on the Internet at this time, the same general rules are likely to apply. Either the user pays directly for access to a book in full text form or a library that has a hard copy (one that can be held in the hands) can make the electronic form available to those the library serves.

Access is one side of the issue of online electronic journals and books. Printing out a copy is another. Reading full text journal articles and books from the monitor is not effective or efficient. The highlighting only lasts while the user is displaying the document on the screen. Writing notes in the margin is difficult and disappears at the speed of the modem connection. Printing or downloading are the solutions. Both have the same problems. Electronic journals and texts will either be printed at the 80 characters per line norm or will require a display formatting software program. Several online journals already require the display formatter program to view the document online. The display formatter program reformats the text into the format of the print copy, which uses columns and includes figures and tables at various points in the text. Without a display formatting program the figures and tables will often be printed at the end of the article because the characters per line feature is set differently. The best known formatter is Acrobat by Adobe. It is available online and can be purchased in many computer software stores or mail order businesses. Documents printed using the reformatter program will be much easier to read and will look similar to the hard copy counterpart.

CHAPTER 23

■■■■■■■■■■■■■■■■■■■■■■■■■■■■■■■■■■

Finding People's E-Mail Addresses

Could it be that a friend from high school who has not been heard from in 20 years has an E-mail address? What if a message could be left for a professor who probably knows the answer to a clinical question if only the right E-mail address could be found? There are ways to locate people and their addresses on the Internet. Seven are discussed below:

1. Old-fashioned direct contact method
2. Online telephone directories
3. World Wide Web search engine
4. E-mail subscriber lists
5. Usenet address server
6. Finger

The old-fashioned method is to call or write the person and ask for his or her E-mail address. It is not creative but often effective and usually results in correct information. Of course, the direct contact method works only if the telephone number or address is known or can be located. If the person lives in the United States and has a mailing address or telephone number, chances are good one or both are contained on a CD-ROM for street addresses or telephone numbers. Both products are available at nearly all computer stores and places that sell computer products. Try PhoneDisc by Powerfinder Pro, Select Phone by ProCD, Street Atlas USA by DeLome Mapping, or Street Wizard by Adept Computer Solutions.

There are also online directories. Many universities and colleges have the names and E-mail address of students and employees listed on their Gopher or Web site. Start with American Universities http://www.clas.ufl.edu/CLAS/american-universities.html. Locate the school of interest and then search the Gopher or Web page for the directory of names. Another source is ClassMates Online. This site lists high school alumni. The uniform resource locator (URL) is http://www.classmates.com/. Reunion Hall is another high school alumni site. The URL is http://www.xscom.com/. If the person's place of work is known, the E-mail address may be listed on the employee roster.

If the person's whereabouts are unknown an online data base may help. The two best known Web sites for addresses, LookUP! and Four 11, have combined to provide better service. The URLs are http://www.lookup.com/ or http://www.four11.com/. Other general directories include American Directory Assistance at http://www.abii.com/lookupusa/adp/peopsrch.htm, Bigfoot at http://bigfoot.com/, Internet Address Finder at http://www.iaf.net, People Finder at http://www.stokesworld.com/peoplefinder/people.html, WhoWhere? at http://www.whowhere.com/, Switchboard at http://switchboard.com/, or World E-Mail Directory at http://www.worldemail.com/. Switchboard boasts the largest directory of more than 90 million names and telephone numbers.

Another approach is to use a search engine such as InfoSeek Guide at http://guide.infoseek.com/. In the second line there is a dropdown window. Select E-mail addresses. Press the search button to the right. On the next screen enter the person's name, city, and state and press Search. In a few seconds the search engine should provide a list of possible E-mail addresses IF the person is listed. If there is no result there are two special help buttons: *e-mail Wizard* that uses fuzzy logic or sign up for *We'll Call You*, which is a free listing so someone can find the user. Hopefully the person the user is trying contact will be trying to contact the user.

The search engine AltaVista also provides access to individuals who have created a Web page or posted to Usenet. Try searching for the individual by contacting AltaVista at http://altavista.digital.com/. Yahoo provides a directory called Netfind at http://www.yahoo.com/text/Reference/White_Pages/Individuals/Netfind.

SavvySearch is a metasearch tool that can send a request to several search engines. The URL is http://www.cs.colostate.edu/~drelling/smartform.html.

If the person being searched for is known to be a member of a particular Listserv, the E-mail address may be available on the list of members. Try sending a message to the Listserv address with a message that says *review* listname *by name*. Be sure to put the name of the list in the space for listname. For example, if the person is a member of the occup-ther Listserv the statement would read: review occup-ther by name.

Another method to locate people is through the Usenet address server, which draws information from Usenet newsgroups. If the person is a member of any newsgroup, chances are good the person's name has been collected by the Usenet address server. To find out, send an E-mail message to Mail-server-rtfm.mit.edu/. Leave the subject line blank. In the body of the message type send usenet-address/name-of-person. For example, if the person's name is Joan Curtis the message would read: send usenet-address/Joan Curtis. The Usenet

Name	Web Site	Freeware or Shareware
TABLE 23-1. PROGRAMS TO HELP LOCATE PEOPLE ON THE INTERNET		
AFinger32	Not given	Freeware
InterSnoop	http://www.akiss.lm.com/	Shareware
NetScan Tools 16 or 32Bit	http://www.eskino.com/~nwps/index.html	Shareware
WSFinger Client for Windows 3.x or 95	http://www.biddeford.com/~jobrien/	Shareware

data base will send back a message with all entries that contain the name specified whether that name appears as part of the user id, the domain name, or just the personal name.

DejaNews can also be used to locate people if they have posted a message on Usenet since March 1995. Type in a name and see if there is an answer.

Several programs are available for PCs that are written to locate people on the Internet (Table 23-1). The names are based on a Unix program called Finger. They are rated as good or better programs and are available from Tucows.

For more information on locating people through the Internet resources read the frequently asked questions at Ohio State. The URL is http://www.cis.ohio-state.edu/hypertext/faq/usenet/finding-addresses/faq.html.

CHAPTER 24

■■■■■■■■■■■■■■■■■■■■■■■■■■■■■■■■■■

Job Hunting and Job Posting

The Internet is an ideal medium for job seekers and employers. Job seekers can look at a broad range of employment opportunities around the world without having to leave home. A single copy of a resumé can be seen and read by hundreds of potential employers, with no stamps required. Employers can post one copy of an employment opportunity that may be read by thousands of potential employees. The announcement can include details, graphics, and even sounds, which would be difficult or impossible in a newspaper want ad or letter. Interviews can be conducted via E-mail, bulletin board services, or chat rooms. No travel expenses, meals, or lodging are necessary. Even background checks can be done through the Internet. Using the Internet, job seekers can learn about the potential employer from current and past employees. Employers can learn about potential employees by engaging people and businesses available in close proximity to the potential employee's home. Some Web sites for job searching are listed in Table 24-1.

All Internet resources can provide avenues for employment. The easiest way to start is to select a search engine and type **employment**. Other possible search terms are jobs, careers, help wanted, job listings, job hunting, job opportunities, job seeking, job services, and the name of the profession such as occupational therapy, physical therapy, speech pathology, vocational rehabilitation, or other rehabilitation specialty. Some Internet resources specialize in providing space for employment opportunities. Usenets, bulletin boards, and the online services all have special groups devoted to employment. For Usenets the best search engine is DejaNews. Right now most of the sites rely on written words but "phone-a-vision" is possible and probably will become common in next few years.

Traditional newspaper want ads are still available for those who are more comfortable with the tried and true. Why not try using **want ads** or **newspaper**

TABLE 24-1. WEB SITES FOR JOB SEARCHING

Name	Web Site
Career Magazine	http://www.careermag.com/careermag/news/
Career Marketing Resumé	http://www.careermarketing.com/
Career Mosaic	http:///www.careermosaic.com/
CareerPath	http://www.careerpath.com/ (newspaper ads)
CareerWeb	http://www.cweb.com/jobs/welcome.html
Chronicle of Higher Education	http://chronicle.merit.edu:8083/.ads/.links.html
College Grad Job Hunter	http://www.collegegrad.com/
Employment Resources	http://alpha.acast.nova.edu/employment.html
Entry Level Job Seeker Asst.	http://members.aol.com/Dylander/jobhome.html
E-Span	http://www.espan.com/
Get a job!	http://www.getajob.com/
IntelliMatch	http://www.intellimatch.com/
Internet Career Connection	http://ccweb.com/
Internet Professional Assn.	http://www.ipa.com/
JobCenter	http://www.jobcenter.com/
JobDirect	http://www.jobdirect.com/
Jobs Library/FedWorld	http://fwux.fedworld.gov/pub/jobs/
JobNet	http://www.westga.edu/~coop/
JobPlace	http://www.jobweb.org/
JobTrak	http://www.jobtrak.com/
JobWeb	http://www.jobweb.com/org/
MedSearch America	http://www.medsearch.com/ (Medical)
Monster Board	http://www.monster.com/
Online Career Center	http://www.occ.com/occ/SearchJobs.html
Online Opportunities	http://www.jobnet.com/
Quest	http://www.questusa.com/(post or search resumés)
Tripod	http://www.tripod.com/work/#services/
Yahoo! Employment Resources	http://www.yahoo.com/business/employment/

and employment on a search engine? Several major newspapers such as the *New York Times* list their want ads online. CareerPath, a Web site, posts the classified ads from several newspapers at http://www.careerpath.com/.

To post a resumé try Quest at http://www.questusa.com. There is no charge if the individual posts the resumé, or Quest posts it for $15. Sample resumés are available for those who need assistance in preparing one.

The biggest matching service is Job Center Employment Services at http://www.jobcenter.com/. The site posts more than 4,000 jobs per week. More than 1,000 people visit the site every day. Major employers can search the data base daily for a fee and can specify exactly what criteria are important in potential employees. Employees can request that their resumé not be viewed by certain employers in case they do not want the current employer to know a job change may be coming. Posting an advertisement costs $10 for 2 weeks. Posting a resumé costs $20 for 6 months. New listings that match the resumé will be sent to the person's E-mail address daily. Matching is accomplished by having the applicant provide key words, which are important, such as the type of job, location, salary, or type of benefits.

The largest medical job search site is MedSearch. It has been advertising jobs in medical fields for several years. For rehabilitation jobs check out http://www.medsearch.com/jobs/catgy/therapy_rehabilitation.html On the day this chapter was written there were want ads for OTR 84, COTA 16, OT Aide 2, PT 108, PTA 7, and SLP 28.

Recruiters are also available on the Internet. If it is easier to pay someone else to do the looking, recruiters will be happy to help. Just use a search engine and type in **recruit**. Most search engines will automatically add various endings such as recruiter, recruiters, recruiting, or recruitments. To be sure, type the search as follows: recruit or recruiter or recruiters or recruiting or recruitment. Others terms are: career placement, job search.

Fraud and misrepresentation are always possible on the Internet. The commercial sites try to limit these problems by screening out employers who are known for questionable business practices such as false or misleading advertisements. However, there is no substitute for doing one's own homework. The Internet is a great way to start a job search or look for applicants but in the final round some old-fashioned methods may still be best. When the search has been narrowed to a select number, a face-to-face interview is still the best guarantee that the person and the employer are as advertised.

Displays 24-1 and 24-2 offer sample Web site entries.

DISPLAY 24-1. WHAT THE WORKER WANTS

Wanted: One job with. . .

Interesting duties that present a "just right" challenge every day

Workplace with lots of neat people to work with on the job and party with after work

Workplace with not too many clients who all appreciate the benefits of a good therapist

Good salary and even better benefits, like 6 weeks paid vacation, unlimited continuing education budget, and a $25,000 sign-on bonus

No requirement to work weekends, evenings, or holidays

Paperwork that is all computerized, forms that are easy to fill out, and a computer that always works

A supervisor who always praises, is never cranky, and helps out anytime things get rough

---

DISPLAY 24-2. WHAT THE EMPLOYER WANTS

Wanted: One employee who. . .

Always comes to work ready to work, arrives on time, and works without complaint

Gets along with everybody and can stop any personality clash before it gets started

Never parties late except at the annual picnic

Doesn't need much money and doesn't care about benefits at all; has no retirement plans, never takes vacation, and always contributes to the United Way appeal

Always has all the paperwork done on time and fixes the computer if it breaks down

Likes the supervisor and visa versa

CHAPTER 25

■■■■■■■■■■■■■■■■■■■■■■■■■■■■■■■■■■■

Telephoning and Faxing

TELEPHONING

Imagine using the Internet to make free long distance calls. As Whoopi Goldberg says, "There's no better savings than free." It is possible, but there are some requirements and some limitations. First, it is possible to get rid of the old telephone for good (Fig. 25-1) and buy the necessary computer equipment. The computer should be running Windows 3.1, Windows 95, or Macintosh System 7.0 or 7.5. In addition, the computer must have a sound card, speakers or a headset, a microphone, a modem, and access to the Internet. So what are the problems? The sound quality may not be consistent or of good quality although good sound boards are available. The difficulty is due to the type of audio signals being transmitted. Second, if the user is paying for an Internet service provider (ISP), the calls are not exactly free. However, because the fee is usually a flat fee per month, the distance of the call is irrelevant.

Internet telephoning works the same way as other applications. When the user requests information, the sending computer selects the information, which is then bundled into packets that are transmitted to the receiving (user's) computer, unbundled, and displayed or played. Telephone calls work in reverse order. The voice message is bundled into packets by the sending (user's) computer and transmitted over the Internet to the receiving computer.

Different telephone programs require different central processing units. Check the requirements on the package. Most require a 486 PC running at 33 MHz or a Mac Performa or PowerMac. The PC will also need a Windows Socket (WinSock) program, which is built into Windows 95 but must be installed for Windows 3.1. Some telephone programs include a WinSock program or an ISP can provide one.

FIGURE 25-1. Make telephone calls without any of these.

Sound cards can have full duplex or half duplex. Full duplex allows the participants to talk and listen to each other at the same time. Telephones provide full duplex. Most sound cards for PCs are half duplex. Participants can talk to each other but not simultaneously (Fig. 25-2). If using the Internet for telephone calls is important, look for a sound card with full duplex such as Creative Labs' Sound Blaster AWE 32. The calls will sound more like regular telephone calls.

Speakers are important but expensive ones are not needed. Prices for adequate speakers range from $40 to $150. The microphone can be purchased for $15 to $20. Some microphones come with headphones. The modem should be at least 14,400 bps; 28,800 is better, and integrated services digital network (ISDN) is best.

The type of Internet connection is not critical for making phone calls. Using a serial line interface protocol, point-to-point protocol, or ISDN connection will not affect the telephone call. Speed of transmission depends in part on the mo-

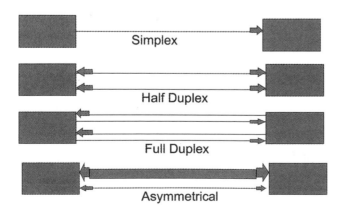

FIGURE 25-2. Types of transmission lines.

TABLE 25-1. WEB SITES FOR TELEPHONE SOFTWARE PROGRAMS		
Name	**Web Site**	**Freeware and Shareware**
CyberPhone	http://www.magenta.com/cyberphone/	Commercial
Internet Call 32-bit	http://dsp.ee.cuhk.edu.hk/proj/icalldl.html	Freeware
Internet Phone	http://www.vocaltec.com/	Demo
IRIS Phone	http://alpha.acad.bf/iris/	Shareware
Microsoft NetMeeting	http://www.microsoft.com/IE/conf/default.htm	Freeware
RoundTable	http://www.ffg.com/rt.html	Shareware
TeleVOX for Windows 95	http://www.voxware.com/index.html	Freeware
WebPhone	http://www.intelco.com/	Commercial
Web Talk	http://www.qdeck.com/	Commercial

dem and choice of Internet connection. ISDN is the fastest. However, the major component of speed is the amount of traffic on the Internet. Afternoon is the busiest time on the Internet. Traffic can be extremely slow even if the user has the best equipment available.

Currently, the best telephone programs are WebPhone by Internet Telephone and WebTalk by Quarterdeck. Others include Cyberphone, by Magenta Communication, and Internet Phone by Vocal Tec. WebPhone allows up to four simultaneous conversations. WebTalk provides two copies of the program so the user can give one to a friend or relative. CyberPhone requires downloading advertisements that appear on the public area server. A private server will not require downloading advertisements but the user must pay for the software. Internet Phone uses Internet relay chat protocol instead of using dedicated servers. Transmission can be poor. Prices range from free (public CyberPhone) to $80 (WebTalk). Software can be purchased in stores or through Web sites listed in Table 25-1.

FAXING

Faxing is actually easier than telephoning because the program usually comes with the modem. Most modems come with two disks. One sets up the modem and the other the fax capability. The fax is usually configured as an E-mail first and then sent to the Internet. Set up the fax utility so it provides a printout of the fax as well as sending the fax. The printout provides a record. Also make sure the setup program creates a header or cover sheet that includes the name, address, and fax number of the user and the recipient plus the transaction time. Including the E-mail address, telephone number, and address is also useful because misdirected files can be redirected or the sender notified of a delivery error. Finally, instructing the program to transmit using fine resolution is important if graphics such as tables, figures, or photos are included. Setting the transmission for text, if the option is available, is usually acceptable for text-only documents. It is important to understand the quality of the fax is partly controlled by the sender and partly controlled by the transmitting and receiving fax machines. If the receiving machine is not in good working order, the sender can do little to improve the resulting printout. If repeating the transaction does not improve the quality of the document, the fault may be on the receiving end. Of course, the primary reason a fax is not received is no paper in the receiving fax machine. The second most common reason is the fax machine is turned off. Many complaints about faxing documents can be averted by knowing the basic causes of problems.

The utility program will require the user to specify the type of printer being used, the name of the drive, and the file where the printer instructions are located. Most often the drive will be c:> and the file will be in the operating system directory or word processing program.

Finally, the user must instruct the program regarding the type of telephone line and dialing instructions. Most often the type is Tone or Touch Tone. The alternative is Rotary. Dialing instructions include the number of attempts the program should make before quitting and the wait between redials. Usually two or three redials within 2 to 3 minutes is sufficient. If the party is not reached during that interval, the party has the line tied up (long transmission or telephone call) and will not be ready to receive for some time. Some fax utilities will also allow the user to set the time for evening or night hours when the receiving fax is less likely to be busy. The disadvantage of night transmission is that the fax may be turned off.

If the user does not have a fax modem, a fax can still be sent using services available via Internet Mail. Some charge a subscription fee and some a per transaction fee; a few are free. The concept is the same. A fax is sent as an E-mail but is delivered as a fax. The fax transmission is using the same line as the Internet connection. While a fax is being sent, or received, the Internet cannot be accessed. Programming the fax utility to send during night hours gives the user more flexibility in using the Internet for other activities.

A fax can be sent anywhere the Internet goes. This means there is good fax capability in North America, Europe, Australia, and Antarctica. South America and Asia have fair capability. Africa, except South Africa, has poor capability. Do not send a fax to Africa unless verification has been made that it can be received.

For more information, the following Internet sites may be useful (Fig. 25-3):

http://www.itsnet.com/commercial/action/fod-list.html (Fax-On-Demand Systems)

http://www.northcoast.com/savetz/fax-faq.html (FAQ—How can I send a fax?)

ftp://rtfm.mit.edu/pub/usenet/news.answers/internet-services/fax-faq

Newsgroup: comp.dcom.fax

Newsgroup: fj.net.fax

FIGURE 25-3. Just the fax!

CHAPTER 26

■■■■■■■■■■■■■■■■■■■■■■■■■■■■■■■■■■■■■■

Safety and Security on the Internet

The tendency is to assume that only the person being addressed in the E-mail will read it. Because privacy of postal mail is a right, many users assume the same is true for E-mail. Nothing could be further from the truth. E-mail is not private. The systems administrators on both the sending and receiving host computers can easily read any E-mail of choice. The systems administrators can read, view, or hear anything on the computer they oversee. So remember not to say anything in an E-mail that would not be said to a person's face. Also remember not to send any E-mail to people that the employer says cannot be contacted during work time. If sending E-mails to friends is not allowed on company time, do not send them. Although the actual writing and sending of the E-mail may go undetected, the exact time and full message will be stored in the host computer. Even erasing the message from the terminal or user's computer will not get rid of the message. It remains available in the host computer and the systems administrator knows how to retrieve it. There are already examples of people losing their jobs over E-mail that should not have been composed and should not have been sent. Word to the wise: Watch your E-mail!

Systems administrators are not the only people who can get access to the information on a computer. Crackers, amateur or professional, can also get into a computer's memory. Whenever a computer is connected to the Internet, it can be a potential target for someone with too much time and curiosity. Although big targets like telephone company computers and military computers are more common targets, they are not the only ones. The Library computer at the senior author's former place of work was cracked. The cracker was not interested in the Library's computer. It houses the library catalog and some administrative files concerning policies and procedures of the library. The cracker was simply using the library catalog to try to get to bigger game. The real target was the Johnson Space Center computers. Fortunately, the security system at the Space Center was not easy to crack, but the library staff learned an important lesson. Any computer can be a target for crackers. As a result of the incident, the systems administrator at the library now requires all employees to change their sign-on password every 3 months to make life a little tougher for hackers. Changing passwords is a good idea. Some people suggest that passwords should not be all letters but should contain a number or two as well. It increases the number of possible combinations.

Because nothing is absolutely safe on a computer that connects to the Internet, one should also consider the risk of sending a credit card number over the Internet. As shopping via the Internet increases, so will the use of credit card transactions. Most companies that accept credit card transactions use an encryption program to scramble the numbers as they are being transferred and then unscramble them at the destination computer (Fig. 26-1). However, the credit card owner should be aware that once again there is no perfect encryption program that cannot be cracked. Once the holes in the encryption are known, it is almost as easy to read credit card numbers from the Internet as it is to stand in front of a public telephone and watch someone push the buttons to use a long distance credit card. The user needs to consider the risk before giving a credit card number over the Internet. As encryption programs improve, the risk may decrease but it is never likely to drop to zero.

The problem of security brings up another issue. How can patient and client records be protected and confidentiality maintained? If a computer with patient or client information on it is also being used to access the Internet, the professional needs to talk with the systems administrator about security. Computer programmers can create what is called a firewall. A firewall is a host computer designed to serve as the first line of defense against crackers. The firewall protects the computer files that are not to be made public while giving access to those that are.

Original Message

> Order No. 4207359
> Credit Card No.
> 0987 6543 3210 9876
> Item No. 225375
> Price $89.95

Data Encryption Key

Encrypted Message

> %$^#& (-) +&*%^$#@
> ^&=\? <!>\ +=
> ^&+) /,({ $]@&[~#/<
> ^&%$ (-) ##*^)%
> (\>*%# &)_+|

FIGURE 26-1. Using an encryption program to secure data.

CHAPTER 27

■■■■■■■■■■■■■■■■■■■■■■■■■■■■■■■■■

Business and Marketing on the Internet

There are three ways to market and advertise on the Internet: the Web, newsgroups, and mailing lists. For most marketing and advertising, the Web is the best.

The four methods of developing a Web page to promote a product or service are:

1. Develop the Web page after learning hypertext markup language and have the Internet service provider (ISP) mount it on his or her server.
2. Have the ISP create the Web page and mount it on the server.
3. Use a Cybermall such as Open Market.
4. Develop a Web page and mount it on the user's computer.

The cheapest way is the first and the most expensive is the last. The expense occurs because a Web site needs to be available all or most of time to be an effective marketing tool. Therefore, a computer will need to be online 24 hours a day with a dedicated line.

There are a number of sites for advertising products on newsgroups. The sites usually focus on one type of product such as computers, bicycles, or science fiction. If products such as books or equipment are for sale, a newsgroup may be useful.

E-mail is not generally a format for advertising, but it can be used for promotional materials. John Brogan wrote a software program called Reply.Net to provide businesses with a method of responding to E-mail requests for customers. Reply.Net is most useful for sending brochures, catalogs, announcements, flyers, fact sheets, or schedules. Reply.Net can be reached by calling 800-210-2220 or 301-930-3011 in the Washington, DC area. The E-mail address is get.info@reply.net.

Some tips on advertising on the Internet are:

1. Advertise only on designated listservs, newsgroups, or individual Web pages. Advertising where it is not permitted or accepted will result in a deluge of messages from irate netters who will not be in a good mood (as in downright angry).
2. Be straightforward and truthful about the advertising. People on the Internet do not like to be misled. Anyone who feels the information is misleading is likely to tell members of several listservs or newsgroups about the experience. The word can spread very quickly on the Internet. It is a part of the Global Village.
3. Provide as much useful information as possible—the more useful, the better. Internet users want information and will visit any site that provides quality.
4. Gather data only with the user's informed consent. Do not deceive the person about the purpose of the data gathering.
5. Do not use or sell the consumer data without user permission.

Doing some homework before starting a Web site or selling anything on the Internet is important. Read other advertisements on newsgroups or Web pages. Print out a copy of those that seem the best. Read about advertising and marketing on newsgroups or Web pages. There are several newsletters and many books about doing business on the Internet. Investing a little time and money in resource materials is well worth the effort.

## CHAPTER 28

Best Internet Sites

MARTINDALE

http://www-sci.lib.uci.edu/HSG/HSGuide.html

The site is maintained by Jim Martindale and Frank Potter at the University of California-Irvine. It is an excellent guide to hundreds of medical sites on the Internet. The focus is on multimedia. They annotate most of the listings. See also Medical Matrix.

MEDICAL MATRIX

http://www.slackimc.com/matrix

This site is a joint project of Dr. Gary Malet and the American Medical Informatics Association (http://amia2.amia.org/). It lists over 1000 resources by various categories such as public policy issues, associations and organizations, and health and medical resources.

MEDWEB: ELECTRONIC NEWSLETTERS AND JOURNALS

http://www.emory.edu/WHSCL/medweb.html

The site is a comprehensive list of medical journals, newsletters, and tables of contents available online. There are two levels: medical specialty and Web sites with good annotations.

MEDWEB DISABILITIES

http://www.gen.emory.edu/medweb/medweb.disabled.html

This is a comprehensive resource for links to newsletters and data bases for persons with disabilities.

NATIONAL LIBRARY OF MEDICINE CATALOG

http://www.nlm.nih.gov/databases/locator.html

This site provides access to the National Library of Medicine catalog including all books, journals, and audiovisuals.

HYPERDOC

http://www.nlm.nih.gov/

This site allows access to the data bases at the National Library of Medicine, including HIV/AIDS, HSTAT, and DIRLINE.

AGENCY FOR HEALTH CARE POLICY RESEARCH

http://text.nlm.nih.gov/ahcpr/guides.html

The site contains the full text of AHCPR's clinical practice guidelines.

VISUAL HUMAN PROJECT

http://www.nlm.nih.gov/research/visible/visible_human.html

This site provides cross-sectional images of an actual cadaver at 1-mm intervals. It also provides links to other anatomy sites.

CENTERS FOR DISEASE CONTROL AND PREVENTION

http://www.cdc.gov/

This site includes the *Morbidity and Mortality Weekly Report* (*MMWR*), the Emerging Infectious Diseases online, and the HazDat (Hazardous Substance Release/Health Effects Database).

REHABDATA

http://www.cais.net/naric/

This data base includes over 46,000 documents. This site only provides access to the results of the most requested topics but they are excellent resources.

ASSISTIVE TECHNOLOGY

http://marin.org/npo/ata/atacenters.html

This is a major assistive technology site.

MUSCLES IN ACTION

http://www.med.umich.edu/lrc/hypermuscle/hyper.html

This interactive multimedia site is designed to teach muscle actions of humans.

PHYSICAL THERAPY

http://www.apta.org/

The page of the American Physical Therapy Association provides a variety of links to sites of interest to physical therapists.

OCCUPATIONAL THERAPY

http://www.mother.com/~ktherapy/ot/

This a major site of interest to occupational therapists with over 350 links. It is maintained by Richard Powell and includes access to Marilyn Ernest-Conibear's data base of occupational therapy literature.

SPEECH PATHOLOGY

http://www.mankato.msus.edu/dept/comdis/kuster2/welcome.html

This offers access to several useful speech pathology sites.

PHYSICAL MEDICINE AND REHABILITATION

http://www.gen.emory.edu/medweb/medweb.rehab.html

This provides access to most major physical medicine and rehabilitation medicine sites. The second best site is http://weber.u.washington.edu/~rehab/.

BOOKS TO BUY

http://www.amazon.com/

This site offers access to 1.25 million book titles.

CHAPTER 29

Dealing With Computer-Related Disorders

Cumulative trauma disorders or repetitive strain injuries occur from repetitive activity such as typing, keyboarding, clicking and dragging a mouse, moving a trackball, or tapping a glide device. Other problems are caused by eye strain, poor or improper posture, and poor positioning. The final result is pain and sometimes surgery.

Three types of injuries are common: tendonitis, tenosynovitis, and carpal tunnel syndrome (CTS). Tendonitis is caused by inflammation of the tendons and may range from mild to severe. It can lead to CTS if not treated. Tenosynovitis is an inflammation of the sheaths surrounding the tendon. It too ranges from mild to severe and may lead to CTS. CTS occurs when the swelling tendons put pressure on the median nerve of the wrist. The National Center for Health Statistics estimates about 1.89 million people suffer from CTS. Many of those affected are using computers. Many assembly-type jobs also involve repetitive activities.

Eye strain occurs for several reasons. The monitor may be too close or too low. The brightness control may be set on an overly bright setting, which can cause blurry characters. The contrast may be set so the letters do not stand out from the background. The choice of colors may not optimize the contrast. The best contrast is black characters on a light gray background. Lighting is also important. Direct sunlight may cause glare by reflecting off the monitor. Incandescent light, fluorescent light, and natural light are all acceptable if they do not reflect off glassy or shiny surfaces. Also, lighting changes during the day and may need to be adjusted according to work needs. Finally, eyes need to change focus length. For 5 minutes of every hour the eyes should be focused on some distant object.

Posture is probably the number one complaint. Back and neck strain are common complaints. The chair, table, keyboard, and monitor need to be adjusted for each person. The height for the chair should create a 90° angle for the hips and knees while the feet are flat on the floor or slightly elevated at the toes. An adjustable backrest and seat can provide adjustments to fit different seating positions. The elbows should be at 90° to the keyboard. A wrist pad can help relieve wrist strain. The monitor should be tilted to between 15° and 30° below the eyes. Be sure the monitor is directly in front of both eyes to avoid neck strain and about 18 to 24 inches away from the eyes.

The environment is also important. The room temperature should be comfortable. Air should be circulating. Plants can help clean the air. If the hands are always cold, check with a physician to determine if circulation problems are present. Stretching and yoga exercises can help relieve stress and reduce pain. Learning to listen to the body is also important. If it hurts, stop doing it. Find another way or adjust something. Options are available. Consultants can help if the problem continues.

Many products have been designed to improve the work environment. Some products can be helpful but do not buy them without trying them. Er-

---

Display 29-1. INTERNET SITES FOR INFORMATION ON COMPUTER-RELATED DISORDERS

Web Sites

Amara's RSI page: http://www.amara.com/aboutme/rsi.html

Typing injuries by Dan Wallach: http://www.cs.princeton,edu/~dwallach/tifaq/general.html

University of Nebraska-Lincoln RSI Page: http://engr-www.unl.edu/ee/eeshop/rsi.html

CDT News by Center of Workplace Health: http://ctdnews.com/

Carpal tunnel syndrome: http://www.sechrest.com/mmg/cts.ctsintro.html

Cornell Theory Center by Alan Hedge: http://www.tc.cornell.edu:80/~hedge/

Mailing Lists

Discussion of repetitive strain injuries: To subscribe, send E-mail to listserv@ucsfm.ucsf.edu with a message in the body "subscribe sorehand yourname"

RSI Network Newsletter: To subscribe, send a request to dadadata@world.std.com

RSI Discussion List: To subscribe send E-mail to listserver@tictac.demon.co.uk with a message in the body to "subscribe rsi-uk" followed by your real name

FTP Sites

ftp://ftp.csua.berkeley.edu/pub/typing-injury/rsi-network

Usenet

misc.health.injuries.rsi.misc—open newsgroup on RSI

misc.health.injuries.rsi.moderated—moderated newsgroup on RSI

gonomically designed equipment is widely available. Some (eg, wrist supports) are not terribly expensive. Other equipment, such as special chairs and work centers, can cost over $500. Insist on trying before buying. There are several types of keyboards. Some may help relieve one kind of strain only to increase another type of strain. Divided keyboards may have the keys too far apart for smaller hands, for example. Sometimes simple adjustments are better and cheaper. A different table, another office chair, or a simple wrist splint can improve performance without expensive equipment changes. The Internet provides many sites that offer information and discussion. Some are listed in Display 29-1.

REFERENCES

Linden, P. (1995). *Compute in comfort: Body awareness training: Day-to-day guide to pain-free computing*. Upper Saddle River, NJ: Prentice Hall PTR.

Mueller, J. (1990). *The workplace workbook: An illustrated guide to job accommodation and assistive technology*. Washington, DC: The Dole Foundation.

Parker, K. G. (1992). *Cumulative trauma disorders: Current issues and ergonomic solutions: A systems approach*. Boca Raton, FL: Lewis Publishers.

Putz-Anderson, V. (Ed). (1988). *Cumulative trauma disorders: A manual for musculoskeletal diseases of the upper limbs*. London: Taylor & Francis.

CHAPTER 30

■■■■■■■■■■■■■■■■■■■■■■■■■■■■■■■■■■■

The Internet of the Future

Although no one knows exactly what will happen as the Internet grows in popularity, certain factors will influence its direction. Among these are some familiar and not so familiar concepts. They include bandwidth, integrated services digital network (ISDN), cable modems, fiberoptics, virtual reality modeling language (VRML), Java, and longer Internet protocol (IP) addresses.

Bandwidth is a measurement of the amount of data that can be transmitted over a particular network circuit in a given period of time. Bandwidth is measured in bits per second (bps). The wider the bandwidth, the more data that can be transferred simultaneously. Currently the bandwidth for most home computers using traditional telephone lines and analog modems stops at 28,800 bps. That speed may be fast enough for text information, but for many multimedia formats 28,800 bps is extremely slow. The ISDN is a new telephone cable that uses special modems that transmit and receive over the Internet faster but at a higher cost. ISDN modems do not have to change the signal from digital to analog and back again, which takes time. The time can then be used to transmit directly from one computer to another using the digital code. However, telephone companies have been slow to upgrade their lines because of the expense, which is then passed onto the customer. Many Internet service providers provide a choice of point-to-point/serial line Internet protocol (PPP/SLIP) connections or ISDN. The rate for PPP/SLIP will be typically be one-third to one-fourth the cost of an ISDN connection. The advantage is that ISDN connections are about four times as fast and can carry the higher quality signals needed to transmit video and audio images. ISDN can transmit data at speeds of up to 128,000 bps.

Cable modems are even faster than ISDN modems because they use the cable networks, not the telephone lines. Cable modems attach computers to networks using the same cabling system that connects television sets to the cable company.

Thus, cable modems could use the big screen television as a monitor. Graphic images could be 54 inches on a big screen television. One drawback is the problem of line noise from radio signals and household appliances plus mouse-clicks that can distort the data and mess up the signal. The Reload button might be working overtime.

Newer cable companies are using fiberoptic cable lines to transmit information. The fiberoptic cables use infrared or visible light rays as the carrier. Data travel on a glass or plastic fiber made from silicon dioxide; the fiber is the diameter of a human hair. Fiberoptic cables are not as affected by line noise. The cable can also have lines going in opposite directions at the same time so that when one direction is blocked it goes the other way. Fiberoptic cables can send information at the rate of 420 mbps (megabits/second). A single fiber can transmit 200 million telephone conversations at the same time.

The Internet offers the telephone and cable companies opportunities to combine services. Consumers may someday be paying one bill to cover telephone, cellular phone, fax, cable television, Internet access, and pay for view. Paying bills will be via bank transfer directed from the computer screen. For people who already own and use computers such ideas seem possible. Software for paying bills via computer is already in use. The widespread acceptance of such bundled services depends on getting computers into as many homes as presently have telephones and televisions. To accomplish that degree of consumer acceptance, computers will need to decrease in cost to below the $1,500 to $2,000 now needed for a basic multimedia system.

Changes in Web page development can be expected. There have already been three versions of Hypertext Markup Language (HTML). However, HTML does not have the capacity to provide animation in real time. Virtual Reality Modeling Language (VRML) does permit the development of animation as well as objects which appear to be three-dimensional. VRML uses a special engine to display the Web page so that animation and three-dimensional environments can be viewed. In the future it is expected that VRML will also provide light and sound to increase the range and realism of the Web pages.

Java is another programming language that can provide animation, but Java also requires a high-end workstation such as Sun Microsystem to create the applications called applets. (JavaScript, however, can be used with Windows 95 or Mac operating systems.) Applets are helper applications designed to run with Java. When Java needs a helper application, it can send an applet with the document file so that there is no problem finding the right application with which to run the file. In other words, if a Telnet program is needed to access a data base listed on a Web page developed using Java, Java will send the Telnet program in the form of an applet so that the user can proceed directly to the data base without having to set up a Telnet program on the hard drive and then tell the Web browser where to find it. JavaScript is available in several Web page creation tools now. Check the software box to see if it is included in the Web page creation program.

Live broadcasts are also likely to become more common on the Internet. Technology such as the CU-SeeMe program already facilitates live broadcasts, but the quality is limited. Better programs or better programmers will improve the quality. As the quality improves, quantity will likely follow. Pay for view may be as close as the nearest access to the Internet. For people living in remote areas where cable is limited or does not exist, Internet access, via telephone lines, may provide an alternative.

Finally, longer Internet addresses are coming and the three letter domains will be history. Longer Internet addresses are needed because the present system is running out of new addresses just when the demand is growing. The present system is based on four sets of three numbers with dots in between. The numbers range from 0 to 255. Thus the last number is the current system is 255.255.255.255 Clearly changing the present numbering system to include numbers up to 999.999.999.999 would help forestall the need for longer numeric addresses, but somewhere along the line those numbers would also run out. To avoid having to add new numbering systems every few years, the system needs to be large enough to provide numbers to every person on earth for the foreseeable future. To achieve that objective, the numbers must be longer. Expect a new longer numbering system soon.

A new numbering system does not mean that everyone will have to learn a new Internet address. The letter combinations most people use are aliases. They can be kept intact as long as they can be associated by the Domain Name Server computer. What is changing is the use of the three letter domain addresses such as edu for education, gov for government, or com for commercial. Because the rest of the world has adopted the two letter codes for countries rather than the three letter codes for types of Internet users, the United States is starting to follow suit. New addresses in the United States end in .us, not one of six three-letter codes. Established address aliases will probably remain since they are already in

FIGURE 30-1. I see you spending many long hours on the Internet.

the Domain Name Server computer, but new requests for addresses will be required to end in the two letters .us

In summary, the Internet is a fast-growing and rapidly changing environment for information access and transfer. Many uses have already been developed, but more uses and improvements in current uses are sure to come. As children learn to use the Internet in school, they will view the Internet as a primary information source that is as fast as a speeding bullet. Using the Internet to locate information will seem as natural to them as using a dictionary to look up a word is to most older adults. In a few years the Internet will be as commonplace as the telephone. People will wonder what life was like before the Internet moved us one step closer to the Global Village. Welcome to the Internet Village (Fig. 30-1).

INTERNET GUIDE TO REHABILITATION RESOURCES

INTRODUCTION

The purpose of this resource guide is to provide some useful starting points for exploring the vast volume of information available on the Internet. The sites listed are only a sample of resources available that may be useful to rehabilitation professionals. A comprehensive list would be out of date before it was published and require a book at least twice as thick. Many useful resources have been left off the list to provide room for a broader list of topics. The reader will quickly locate additional sources by clicking on links to other pages identified on the ones listed below. Sites with many links have been intentionally listed to provide such additional resources.

This list of resources was compiled using the Netscape Web browser and selected search engines, especially Hot Bot, AltaVista, and InfoSeek. Much of the compilation was done at the Louisiana State University (LSU) Medical Center in New Orleans. While compiling this resource guide, the rapid growth and change of the Internet became evident because universal resource locators (URLs) were added and changed during the compilation process. Undoubtedly, these changes will continue during the interim between publication and purchase. Therefore, it is important for the reader to recognize that some URLs will be changed or disappear. Fortunately, many Webmasters provide links to the new pages and search engines can be used to locate other sources to replace those that are lost.

Mailing Lists via E-mail (Listserv, Mailbase, Mailserv, Majordomo, and Newsletters)

Information for subscribing to the mailing lists is written as follows: The name of the mailing list is typed between the lesser and greater signs (<>). Do not type the signs when addressing the E-mail. Type only the E-mail address. The exact wording of the message is typed between quotation marks. Do not type the quotation marks in the actual message. Type only the message. Example: To subscribe to the Occup-ther listserv the E-mail might look as follows:

To: occup-ther-request@ac.dal.ca
From: kittyr@library.tmc.edu
Message: subscribe Kathlyn Reed

Usenets

The best source of information on the Usenets is to search the Web site DejaNews at http://www.dejanews.com. It has the largest collection of indexed archived Usenets available.

Art Therapy

 American Art Therapy Association (AATA)

http://www.louisville.edu/groups/aata-www/

Major site for art therapy information and source materials including information about AATA, membership application, upcoming conferences, and state art therapy association.

 Art Therapy in Canada

http://home.ican.net/~phansen.index.html

 Art Therapy on the Web

http://www.sofer.com/art-therapy/

This home page contains references to numerous pages of interest to art therapists, including an introduction to art therapy on the Web, art therapy links, and art therapy vacancies.

Contact: Danny Sofer, Webmaster danny@sofer.com

 ARTTHX-L

Address E-mail to <LISTSERV@listserv.aol.com>. Leave subject line blank. In message space type one line "SUBSCRIBE ARTTHX-L youremailaddress yourfirstname yourlastname." Includes separate pages on art therapy with children, for bereavement issues, and with adults. Also provides information about the profession of art therapy, the education and training required, conferences and meetings, and the professional association in Canada.

sci.psychology.psychotherapy

No specific Usenet. Some discussion in this Usenet.

COALITIONS

 Activity Therapy Innovations (ATI)

http://ourworld.compuserve.com/homepages/ATI/

ATI is a nonprofit organization designed to bring together various activity therapies in a cooperative effort to improve the professions.

 Expressive Therapy Concepts

http://membrane.com/graphic.html

A nonprofit organization dedicated to education and service to the creative arts therapies and related disciplines.

 National Coalition of Arts Therapies Associations (NCATA)

http://membrane.com/ncata/

Web page for the NCATAs that includes the American Association for Music Therapy, American Art Therapy Association, American Dance Therapy Association, National Association for Drama Therapy, American Society for Group Psychotherapy & Psychodrama, and the National Association for Poetry Therapy.

Communication Disorders: Major Resources

 ### American Speech-Language-Hearing Association (ASHA)

http://www.asha.org/

This Web site is a resource for ASHA members, persons interested in information about communication disorders, and those wanting career and membership information.

Contact: webmaster@asha.org

 ### International Clinical Phonetics and Linguistics Association (ICPLA)

http://tpowel.comdis.lsumc.edu/icpla/icpla.htm

The ICPLA Web site includes information on ICPLA officers and membership, previous and upcoming symposia, and publications such as *Clinical Linguistics and Phonetics*, a newsletter, and *Pathologies of Speech and Language* with table of contents and ordering information.

Contact: Thomas W. Powell, Webmaster Tpowel@lsumc.edu

 ### MedWeb-Hearing

http://www.gen.emory.edu/medweb/medweb.hearing.html

Good resources for audiologists.

 ### Net Connections for Communication Disorders and Sciences

http://www.mankato.msus.edu/dept/comdis/kuster2/welcome.html

This Net Connections Web site is one of the largest and best Web sites on communication disorders information. It contains hundreds of resources including discussion groups (Listserv, Majordomo, Mailbase, Listproc), Usenet (newsgroups), E-journals and publications, Gopher sites, FTP sites, Telnet sites, World Wide Web (WWW), WAIS (wide area information server), online information about university programs, and commercial and nonprofit items of interest to communication disorders and sciences personnel.

Contact: Judith Maginnis Kuster, Webmaster kuster@vax1.mankato.msus.edu

L   **ASHA-AUD-FOCUS**

asha-aud-focus@ncm.com
Note: ASHA members only.

L   **ASHA-AUD-FORUM**

asha-aud-forum@ncm.com
Note: ASHA members only.

L   **ASHA-AUD-HEADLINES**

asha-aud-headlines@ncm.com
Note: ASHA members only.

L   **CDMAJOR**

cdmajor@kentvm.kent.edu OR cdmajor@kentvm.bitnet
listserv@kentvm.kent.edu
"subscribe cdmajor yourfirstname yourlastname"

L   **CNET-ANN**

cnet-ann@listserv.arizona.edu

L   **CNET-STD**

cnet-ann@lstserv.arizona.edu

L   **COMMDIS**

commdis@rpitsvm.bitnet OR commdis@vm.its.rpti.edu

GRNDRNDS

grndrnds@wvnvm.wvnet.edu

COMMUNICATION DISORDERS: OTHER RESOURCES

 Speech Language Pathology and Related Web Sites

http://webpages.marshall.edu/~searls1/slplinks.htm

Provides links to a number of sites of interest to speech pathologists.

 Ultra Oral Imaging Laboratory

http://www.cc.nih.gov/rm/sp/

Laboratory of the Speech-Language Pathology section of the Department of Rehabilitation Medicine at The National Institutes of Health (NIH) that focuses on the use of ultrasound as a diagnostic tool for speech and swallowing disorders.

 University Programs in Speech-Language Pathology and Audiology

http://www.uww.edu/commdis/cdprograms.html

This University Programs Web site lists programs in speech-language pathology (SLP), audiology (A), or both (SLP/A) by state with links to those with a WWW site. It also identifies which programs are certified by the Council on Academic Accreditation of the American Speech-Language Hearing Association (ASHA).

Contact: Scott Bradley, PhD, Webmaster bradleys@uwwvax.uww.edu

Creative Arts Group Therapist

 GROUPTALK

Address E-mail to <majordomo@albie.wcupa.edu>. Leave subject line blank. In message space type one line "subscribe grouptalk."

Dance Therapy

 American Dance Therapy Association

http://www.citi.net/ADTA/

Describes the activities of the American Dance Therapy Association (ADTA)

 Denny's Page

http://www.prairienet.org/~dmb

Provides information about dance and movement therapy.

 ADTA ListServ

Address E-mail to <ListProc@list.ab.umd.edu>. In subject line type ADTA. In message space type one line "subscribe ADTA yourfirstname yourlastname." Send message.

 misc.health.alternative, rec.music.industrial

No specific Usenet. Some discussion in these Usenets.

Drama Therapy

 Drama Therapy

http://csep.sunyit.edu/~joel/nadt.html

Provides information from published material about the National Association for Drama Therapy (NADT), requirements to become a drama therapist, membership categories in NADT, and upcoming conferences, but is not NADT's home page.

Horticultural Therapy

 American Horticultural Therapy Association (AHTA)

http://aggie-horticulture.tamu.edu/horther/ahta.html

Describes the national association and its activities.

 Horticultural Therapy—I Can Garden

http://www.icangarden.com/special-interest/hortther.htm

Good description of horticultural therapy.

 Horticultural Therapy Links

http://www4.ncsu.edu/eos/users/k/kdmuelle/public/Hort-therapy/ht.html

 Horticultural Therapy Resources

http://www.nchrtm.okstate.edu/webfiles/hort_therapy.html

Music Therapy

 Byung-Chuei Choi's Music Therapy Homepage

http://falcon.cc.ukans.edu/~memt/mt.html

Information on music therapy from one of the major training programs in music therapy—the University of Kansas.

 Canadian Association for Music Therapy (CAMT)

http://www.bmts.com/~smacnay/camt/camt.html

Includes numerous items of interest to music therapists and links to other sites.

Dirk Cusbenbery's Music Therapy Page

http://falcon.cc.ukans.edu/~dirkcush/

A useful site that includes a list of schools and directors of programs in music therapy.

 Music Therapy Schools

http://falcon.cc.ukans.edu/~memt/school.html

 National Association for Music Therapy (NAMT) Homepage

http://www.namt.com/namt/

Provides information about the attributes of music therapy, the professional music therapist, locating a music therapist, finding a job as a music therapist, and information on conferences and activities of the National Association for Music Therapy (NAMT).

Contact: info@namt.com

 Musthp-l

Address E-mail to <listserv@ukanum.cc.ukas.edu>. Leave subject line blank. In message space type one line "subscribe musthp-l yourfirstname yourlastname."

 bit.listserv.autism

No specific Usenet. Some discussion in this Usenet.

Occupational Therapy: Major Resources

 ### InternOT: Occup@tional Ther@py on the Internet

http://alize.ere.umontreal.ca:80/~weisslar/

The InternOT Web site is the largest and best international site for occupational therapy, with hundreds of links to Internet resources for occupational therapy. It is housed at the University of Montreal so, in addition to English, it has some information for French-speaking OT personnel.

Contact: Rhoda Weiss-Lambrau, Webmaster weisslar@alize.ere.umontreal.ca

 ### Occupational Therapy Home Page

http://www.aota.org/

This web site is sponsored by the American Occupational Therapy Association (AOTA) and Foundation (AOTF) and contains information for AOTA members (occupational therapists, assistants, and students), prospective students, and consumers. E-mail addresses for the AOTA staff and positions are listed at http://aota.org/emailadd.html

Contact: pressta@aota.org

 ### Occupational Therapy (OT) Internet World

http://www.mother.com/~ktherapy/ot/

The OT Internet World web site is one of the largest and best sites for occupational therapy in the United States. It has a list of occupational therapy schools sites in the United States and international schools, with links to their Web pages and E-mail addresses. It also has OT DBASE journal abstracts, an edition of The OT Internet directory, and links to hundreds of other resources.

Contact: Richard L. Powell, MA, OTR, Webmaster ktherapy@mother.com

 ### OT-ONLINE: Internet Resources for Occupational Therapist

http://www.dartmouth.edu/~lmlevine/kristin/OTONLINE.html

OT-ONLINE lists newsletters, newsgroups, Web pages, listservs and information on how to develop your own Web page.

Contact: Kristin Levine, Webmaster kristin.levine@valley.net

OTPT Pages (Occupational Therapy and Physical Therapy at Puget Sound)

http://otpt.ups.edu/Rehabilitation/home.html

The OTPT Pages Web site at the University of Puget Sound in Tacoma, Washington was the FIRST web site for OT and PT, and it is still one of the largest and best sites in the United States on the Internet. It has hundreds of links to resources for OT and PT.

Contact: Ron Stone, Webmaster stone@ups.edu

 Occup-ther

Address E-mail to <occup-ther-request@ac.dal.ca>. Leave subject line blank. In message space type one line "subscribe occup-ther yourfirstname yourlastname." Send message. List owner is Barbara O'Shea. Note: This list is for therapists only. Students are not eligible. See the mailing list OTS-List.

 Occupational-therapy

Address E-mail to <mailbase@mailbase.ac.uk>. Leave subject line blank. In message space type one line "JOIN occupational-therapy yourfirstname yourlastname." Send message. Note: This is a British mailing list.

 OT-EDUC

Address E-mail to <listserv@edtech.tekotago.ac.nz>. Leave subject line blank. In message space type one line "subscribe ot-educ yourfirstname yourlastname." Send message. Or, use the OT ONLINE Electronic Mailing List MailServ at http://www.dartmouth.edu/~mlevine/kristin/otlists.html.

 OT-EDUC digest

Address E-mail to <listserv@edtech.tekotago.ac.nz>. Leave subject line blank. In message space type one line "subscribe ot-educ-digest yourfirstname yourlastname." Send message, or use the OT ONLINE Electronic Mailing List MailServ. This is the summarized form of OT-EDUC for busy people who do not want to read every message sent to the Listserv but are interested in the subjects discussed.

OT-GERI

Address E-mail to <majordomo@dartmouth.edu>. Leave subject line blank. In message space type one line "subscribe ot-geri yourfirstname yourlastname." Send message, or use the OT ONLINE Electronic Mailing List MailServ. For digest form, message should read "subscribe ot-geri-digest yourfirstname yourlastname." Send message.

Contact: Kristin Levine kristin.levine@valley.net.

 OT-ONLINE Newsletter

Address E-mail to <majordomo@dartmouth.edu>. Leave subject line blank. In message space type one line "subscribe ot-online yourfirstname yourlastname." Send message, or use the OT ONLINE Electronic Mailing List MailServ. This is a monthly online newsletter.

Contact: Kristin Levine, Editor kristin.levine@valley.net.

 OT-PEDS

Address E-mail to <majordomo@dartmouth.edu>. Leave subject line blank. In message space type one line "subscribe ot-peds yourfirstname yourlastname." Send message, or use the OT ONLINE Electronic Mailing List MailServ. For digest form message should read "subscribe ot-peds-digest."

Contact: Kristin Levine kristin.levine@valley.net

 OT-PSYCH

Address E-mail to <majordomo@dartmouth.edu>. Leave subject line blank. In message space type one line "subscribe ot-psych yourfirstname yourlastname." Send message, or use the OT ONLINE Electronic Mailing List MailServ. For digest form, message should read "subscribe ot-psych-digest."

Contact: Kristin Levine kristin.levine@valley.net.

 OTS-List

Address E-mail to <mailserv@ac.dal.ca>. Leave subject line blank. In message space type one line "subscribe ots-list yourfirstname yourlastname." Send message. List owner is Barbara O'Shea. Note: This mailing list is for students only.

misc.health.therapy.occupational

All areas of occupational therapy.

 sci.med.occupational

This Usenet is for repetitive strain injuries but includes some discussion of occupational therapy.

OCCUPATIONAL THERAPY: OTHER RESOURCES

 Association of Occupational Therapists in Mental Health (AOTMH)

http://www.iop.bpmf.ac.uk/home/trust/ot/aotmh.htm

This Web site contains information of interest to AOTMH members, as well as consumers and others interested in mental health.

 British Columbia Society of Occupational Therapists (BCSOT)

http://www.interchg.ubc.ca/bcsot/

This Web site contains information for BCSOT members, consumers, and others interested in occupational therapy. It also has a list of individuals qualified to offer workshops.

Contact: bcsot@unixg.ubc.ca

 Committee of Occupational Therapists for the European Communities (COTEC)

http://www.santel.lu/HANDITEL/associations/cotec.html

This site contains a list of names and contact information for members of the COTEC.

Occupational Therapy (OT) Internet Directory

http://otpt.ups.edu/Rehabilitation/OT-Directory.html (and)

http://www.mother.com/~ktherapy/ot/otdirsub.htm

The OT Internet Directory Web site is an international listing of occupational therapists, assistants, and students who have requested (via ktherapy web site submission form) to have their names and E-mail address(es) included in the directory. They are listed alphabetically with their E-mail address and other information identified.

Contacts: Coeditors, Sandra Cunningham, PhD, OTR scunni@nomvs.lsumc.edu and Amy Perchick, OTR aperchick@aol.com

Occupational Therapy Programs Accredited by the Accreditation Council for Occupational Therapy Education (ACOTE)

http://www.aota.org/eduprog.html

Lists all occupational therapy and occupational therapy assistant programs accredited by ACOTE or those which have applied for accreditation and have accepted students.

Occupational Therapy Schools Web Pages

http://www.mother.com/~ktherapy/ot/ot-sch.htm

This site includes a complete list and links to U.S. educational programs in occupational therapy, U.S. occupational therapy assistant programs, international schools of occupational therapy, and specific programs/schools with links to their home page Web sites.

Contact: Richard L. Powell, Webmaster ktherapy@mother.com

Occupational Therapy TalkBack

http://www.seagull.net/whitson/ot/talkback2.html

A site for students to share information and ask questions about occupational therapy.

Contact: Tami Whitson whitson@earthlink.net (or) ottalkback@usa.net

OTDBASE Abstracts/OT Internet World

http://www.mother.com/~ktherapy/ot/otd-abs.htm

This site contains a data base of abstracts from all major occupational therapy journals. Marilyn Ernest-Conibear, MA, OT(C) placed this abbreviated search of abstracts from her OTDBASE on this Web site. It contains more than 750 OTD-BASE abstracts under 18 title subjects.

Contact: Richard Powell, Webmaster ktherapy@mother.com

 Sensory Integration International (SII)

http://home.earthlink.net/~sensoryint/

This site contains information of interest to SII members and others interested in sensory integration.

Contact: Staci Wilson, Webmaster sensoryint@earthlink.net

Physical Therapy: Major Resources

 American Physical Therapy Association (APTA)

http://www.apta.org/

This site has information of interest to APTA members about the organization, services provided to members, conferences, and publications. It also contains information of interest to consumers of physical therapy and individuals interested in becoming a physical therapist or assistant.

Contact: Webmaster webmaster@apta.org

 APTA SECTION ON GERIATRICS

http://geriatricspt.org/

This site contains information for APTA members and others with a special interest in geriatrics. It includes a section on geriatrics information and directory, publications and journals, upcoming conferences and events, consumer information, and other health and geriatric-related Internet sites.

Contact: Webmaster geriweb@geriatricspt.org

Physical Therapy: The Web Space

http://www.ualberta.ca/~jdoree/tws.html

This Web page provides links to physical therapy schools, job listings, organizations, literature, disorders, and pages related to physical therapy.

Contact: Webmaster jim.doree@pobox.com

 Physiotherapy Global-Links

http://www.netspot.unisa.edu.au/cgi-bin/pt/home.pl

The Physiotherapy Global-Links Web site at the University of South Australia is a large international physical therapy Web site. It identifies and links to information in the following areas: "What's New" and conference announcements, FTP archive, journal abstracts and articles, employment opportunities, courseware, research groups, mailing lists, images and data base, physiotherapy schools and courses, newsgroups, and other physiotherapy Web sites.

Contact: Webmaster Allan.Christie@unisa.edu.au

 NEUROMUS

Address E-mail to <listserv@sjuvm.st.johns.edu>. Leave subject line blank. In message space type one line "subscribe NEUROMUS yourfirstname yourlastname." Send message. This is APTA's Neurology Section mailing list on neuromuscular aspects of motor performance.

 PHYSIO

Address E-mail to <mailbase@mailbase.ac.uk>. Leave subject line blank. In message space type one line "JOIN physio yourfirstname yourlastname." Send message. This is the British mailing list.

 P-THER

Address E-mail to <majordomo@majordomo.srv.ualberta.@ Leave subject line blank. In message space type one line "SUBSCRIBE P-THER youremailaddress." Send message. This is a general mailing list on all aspects of physical therapy.

PTEDUC

Address E-mail to <pteduc-request@estel.uindy.edu>. Leave subject line blank. In message space type one line "subscribe PTEDUC yourfirstname yourlastname." Send message. This is APTA's Section on Education mailing list.

 RESNA

Address E-mail to <listserv@sjuvm.stjohns.edu> Leave subject line blank. In message space type one line "subscribe RESNA yourfirstname yourlastname." Send message. This the rehabilitation technology organization Rehabilitation Technology Society of North America.

 misc.health.therapy.occupational

No specific Usenet. Some discussion in this Usenet.

PHYSICAL THERAPY: OTHER RESOURCES

 Accredited Programs (USA)

http://www.apta.org/education/index.html

This site has a list of physical therapy programs (Bachelor, Certificate, and Master's) accredited by the Commission on Accreditation on Physical Therapy (CAPT), with links to programs with Web sites.

Contact: Webmaster webmaster@apta.org

 Physiotherapy Schools/Physiotherapy Global-Links

http://www.netspot.unisa.edu.au/pt/schools.html

The Physiotherapy Schools Web site lists programs in Australia, Japan, New Zealand, the United Kingdom, Canada, and the United States, including a link to the accredited programs listed above.

Contact: Webmaster Allan.Christie@unisa.edu.au

Rehabilitation Counseling: Major Resource

 Unofficial Rehabilitation Counseling Web Page

http://pages.prodigy.com/rehabilitation-counseling/index.htm

This is the ONLY MAJOR Web site for rehabilitation counseling. It has information on for prospective students, the Council on Rehabilitation Education (CORE) accredited programs, with link to undergraduate and graduate pages, as well as links to other information on the Certified Rehabilitation Counselor (CRC) examination. It also has information of interest to rehabilitation counselors and the addresses of rehabilitation counseling organizations, none of which as yet have Web sites at press time.

Contact: John D. Rasch, PhD, CRC, Webmaster Rasch@luna.cas.usf.edu

Therapeutic Recreation

 American Therapeutic Recreation Association

http://www.atra-tr.org/

Site provides information about the association and its activities.

 National Recreation & Parks Association

http://www.nrpa.org/

 The Recreation Therapy Home Page

http://152.30.12.86/hhp/students/jeffmansfield/rt.html

Designed for students in recreation therapy.

Contact: Jeffory A. Menstidd, Webmaster jm9690@wcu.edu

 Research Therapeutic Recreation

http://www.pacificnet.net/trresrch.htm

This page provides information and links to research in therapeutic recreation.

Therapeutic Recreation Directory: Activity and Treatment Ideas

http://www.pacificnet.net/computrnet/tractv.htm

Provides information on creative therapeutic recreation activities for use in TR programs.

Contact: Charles Dixon, Webmaster dixon@computnet.com

Therapeutic Recreation TR Said, RT Said Bulletin Board

http://www.pacificnet.net/computrnet/board/index.htm

Read the frequently asked questions and TR Bulletin Policy before posting a question to the Therapeutic Recreation Bulletin Board.

Therapeutic Recreation Directory: Conference & Workshops

http://www.pacificnet.net/computrnet/trconf.htm

Lists therapeutic recreation and recreation conferences and workshops held throughout the United States, Canada, and the world.

Therapeutic Recreation Directory

http://www.pacificnet.net/computrnet/index.htm

A major resource page for practicing therapeutic recreation specialists for ideas and techniques.

Therapeutic Recreation FAQ

http://www.io.org/~xavier/tr.html

Provides answers to questions frequently asked about the field of therapeutic recreation in Canada.

Therapeutic Recreation Network Station

http://www.pacificnet.net/computrnet/trindv.htm

Provides names of individuals with expertise in a variety of therapeutic recreation topics. Individuals can add their names and area of expertise.

 STROL

Address E-mail to <majordomo@indiana.edu>. Leave subject blank. In message space type one line "subscribe strol." This list is for students in therapeutic recreation.

 alt.rec.therapeutic

All aspects of recreational therapy.

 bit.listserv.tbi-support

Some discussion in this Usenet.

GOVERNMENTAL RESOURCES

General Governmental Resources

 AT&T Business Network: Government Bookmarks

http://www.bnet.att.com/government/

The AT&T Business Government Bookmarks identifies and links to the home pages of the 50 states and other state resources. It also identifies and links to the executive, legislative, and judicial branches of government and other Federal resources, including the U.S. Copyright Office. It also lists and links to political committees under politics.

 **YAHOO!: Government**

http://www.yahoo.com/government/

This Government subcategory listing lists hundreds of Federal (executive, legislative, and judicial branches, as well as the military, and intelligence agencies, documents and policy, institutes and research labs), U.S. state, as well as other country and international organizations. It also provides email forms for the President, Vice President, senators, and representatives.

Specific Governmental Resources

 THOMAS: Legislative Information on the Internet

http://thomas.loc.gov/

Full text of federal legislation.

 The United States Senate

http://www.senate.gov/

The U.S. Senate World Wide Web service provides public access to legislative information as well as information about members, committees, and organizations of the Senate and to other U.S. government information resources.

Contact: Webmaster webmaster@scc.senate.gov

 U.S. House of Representatives Home Page

http://www.house.gov/

The U.S. Representatives' World Wide Web service provides public access to legislative information as well as information about members, committees, and organizations of the House and to other U.S. government information resources.

Welcome to the White House

http://www.whitehouse.gov/WH/Welcome.html

The White House World Wide Web site contains information and E-mail access to the President, Vice President, and First Lady. It provides information on What's New, an Interactive Citizens' Handbook, White House history and tours, the virtual library, the briefing room, the White House help desk, the White House for kids, and a White House electronic guest book.

Contact: Webmaster feedback@www.whitehouse.gov

Government Agencies, Centers, and Department Resources

 ## Centers for Disease Control and Prevention (CDC)

http://www.cdc.gov/

Provides information on infectious diseases and publishes the *MMWR* (*Morbidity and Mortality Weekly Report*), a publication that reports statistics and tracks infectious disease outbreaks and control.

 ## Department of Education (DOE)

http://www.ed.gov/

 ## Department of Health and Human Services (DHHS Agencies)

http://www.os.dhhs.gov/

 ## Department of Veterans Affairs (VA)

http://www.va.gov/

FedWorld Information Network

http://www.fedworld.gov/

The FedWorld Information Network site contains FTP sites for government information, documents and files, and FedWorld-Hosted Web sites. It also contains a Federal job announcements and provides additional information and U.S. government information servers.

 Health Care Financing Administration (HCFA)

http://www.hcfa.gov/

 Internet Grateful Med

http://igm.nlm.nih.gov/

Note: To use Grateful Med requires a password.

 Library of Congress

http://lcweb.loc.gov/

 National Cancer Institute (NCI)

http://www.nci.nih.gov/

 National Health Information Center (NHIC)

http://nhic-nt.health.org/

 National Institute on Disability and Rehabilitation Research (NIDRR)

http://www.ed.gov/offices/OSERS/NIDRR/

National Institutes of Health (NIH)

http://www.nih.gov/

National Library of Medicine Health Services/Technology Assessment Text (H STAT)

http://text.nlm.nih.gov/

The H STAT World Wide Web service contains clinical practice guidelines.

National Science Foundation (NSF)

http://www.nsf.gov/

Occupational Safety and Health Administration (OSHA; Department of Labor)

http://www.osha.gov/

Provides information on federal standards for safety and health on the job.

NIHGDE-L

listserv@list.nih.gov

"subscribe nihgde-l yourfirstname yourlastname" Listserv for Table of Contents to NIH Guide.

NIHTOC-L

listserv@jhuvm.hcf.jhu.edu

"subscribe nihtoc-l yourfirstname yourlastname" Listserv for NIH Guide to Grants and Contracts.

OTHER HEALTH AND DIAGNOSIS/DISABILITY RESOURCES

General Resources

 Achoo: Human Life Directory

http://www.achoo.com/achoo/human/index.htm

The Achoo Human Life Directory identifies structures and functions of the human body, human health, human diseases, and human behavior and experience.

 Human Genome Program

http://www.er.doe.gov/production/oher/hug_top.html

This Web site provides lists and links to major sources of information and centers concerned with the project.

 National Rehabilitation Information Center (NARIC)

http://www.cais.net/naric/home.htm

This site includes ABLEDATA, ADA Guide, NARIC publications including the latest NIDRR program directory. It also contains other resources including information and links to NARIC's Bookmarks: lists of disability-, health-, and rehabilitation-related sites, links on the WWW, REHABDATA Index and Search, and Web pages for NIDRR projects. It also contains information on FAR and conferences, and employment opportunities.

 Neurosciences on the Internet

http://www.neuroguide.com

This Web site has general information on getting started exploring Internet sites and searching tips, and neurosciences resources (including information on academic centers, professional organizations and meetings, software, electronic journals, information on human neurologic diseases, newsgroups and Web forums, neurosciences mailing lists, and other resources).

Contact: Neil A. Busis, M.D., Webmaster nab@telerama.lm.com

YAHOO!: Health

http://www.yahoo.com/Health/

The YAHOO! Health web site includes thousands of listings in various subcategories, including alternative medicine, death and dying, disabilities, diseases and conditions, education, employment, fitness, general health, geriatrics and aging, health care, medicine, men's health, mental health, nursing, reproductive health, and women's health, among others.

Yanoff's Internet Services List

http://www.spectracom.com/islist/

This site identifies and links to biology (genetics resources), computers (Internet tools/goodies), dictionaries (*Roget's Thesaurus*, Webster's), disability, employment, health, and medical Internet sources. It is a Magellan 3 Star Site.

Assistive Technology Resources

ABLEDATA: The National Database of Assistive Technology Information

http://www.abledata.com/

The ABLEDATA project is funded by the National Institute on Disability and Rehabilitation Research (NIDRR), U.S. Department of Education. This Web site identifies what ABLEDATA is, ways to access ABLEDATA, purchase of the ABLEDATA data base, online Versions, ABLEDATA and NARIC, new ABLE-DATA service feature, and ABLEDATA user products and services.

Alliance for Technology Access (ATA)

http://www.ataccess.org/

The ATA helps to enhance the lives of people with disabilities through technology, by raising public awareness, implementing initiatives, and providing information and hands-on exploration at community resource center. The site contains an ATA profile and information on their book and locations of the ATA resource centers, a list of vendors, success stories, FAR, links to other great Web sites, as well as WWW design to ensure access for people with disabilities and access to the WWW.

Webmaster atainfo@ataccess.org

 Assistive Technology for People With Mental Retardation

http://thearc.org/faqs/assistqa.html

 Assistive Technology Online

http://www.asel.udel.edu/at-online/

 Disability Connection

http://www2.apple.com/disability/welcome.html

This Apple disability Web site identifies various Apple resources available to explore Macintosh assistive technology solutions from Apple's Worldwide Disability Solutions Group. Macintosh assistive technology resources for individuals with disability, including resource sheets, data bases, shareware and freeware software from Apple, as well as disability-related Web pages. It also provides information about Convomania, an Apple-sponsored Internet hangout in hospitals, camps, Ronald McDonald Houses, and homes.

 The Hub: For Information for People in Wheelchairs

http://www.inch.com/~dog666/hub/

Provides information about wheelchairs, travel, and much more.

 IBM Special Needs Solutions

http://www.austin.ibm.com/sns/index.html

This Web site identifies IBM Independence Series trademark assistive devices and software tools as a way to enhance the education, employability, and quality of life of people with disabilities by making the computer more accessible and friendly to people with vision, hearing, speech, mobility, and attention/memory disabilities. It includes product and ordering information.

RESNA Technical Assistance Project

http://www.resna.org/resna/

The Rehabilitation Engineering and Assistive Technology Society of North America (RESNA) operates these projects and programs under the Technology-Related Assistance for Individuals With Disabilities Act Amendments of 1994 (P.L. 103–218) or "Tech Act." The National Institute on Disability and Rehabilitation Research (NIDRR) of the U.S. Department of Education (DOE) administers the program. The 56 National Tech Act projects funded under this grant are listed, and examples of services these projects may provide are identified. Information on assistive technology and the RESNA TA project and staff, legislative resources, reference library, assistive technology job bank, a calendar of events, and Internet assistive technology resources are given.

Contact: Todd H. Miller tmiller@resna.org

Associations for Persons With Disabilities Resources

 ## American Association of People With Disabilities (AAPD)

http://www.aapd.com/

This Web site identifies benefits (including access to insurance and a newsletter), how to sign up to become a member (for $10 and anyone can join if you want to support an organization that helps people help themselves), and other information and news of interest to members. It also lists other sites and requests feedback.

 ## Disabled Peoples' International (DPI)

http://www.escape.ca/~dpi/index.html

International organization for persons with disabilities that supports efforts to promote human rights for people with disabilities, publishes a journal *Disability International*, and provides information and news about disability.

National Association of Developmental Disabilities Councils (NADDC)

http://www.igc.apc.org/NADDC/

NADDC promotes national policy enabling individuals with developmental disabilities to have the opportunity to make choices regarding the quality of their lives and community involvement.

Diagnosis/Disability Resources

Note: This is only a sampling of the resources available. There are many, many more.

ABUSE

 ### alt.abuse.recovery

Support for persons recovering from abuse.

ADDICTIONS

 ## National Clearinghouse for Alcohol and Drug Information

http://www.health.org/

Government site on substance abuse, addictions, and prevention.

 ## Recovery HomePage

http://www1.shore.net/~tcfraser/recovery.htm

Provides the largest number of resources on addiction on the Internet.

 ## Web of Addictions

http://www.well.com/user/woa/

Provides accurate information about many types of addiction, offers a number of articles, and points to links to other sites dealing with addiction.

AIDS/HIV

 AIDS Treatment Data Network

http://www.aidsnyc.org/network/index.html

The Network is a nonprofit community-based organization providing treatment, counseling, and referrals. It includes information about treatments for HIV and AIDS, a directory of clinical trials, the Access Project, treatment review, "In the News," PHS guidelines, a glossary of drugs and opportunistic infections and conditions, and alternative treatment. It also provides links to other HIV/AIDS Internet sites.

 Center for AIDS Prevention Studies (CAPS)

http://chanane.ucsf.edu/capsweb/

This Center at the University of California San Francisco is committed to maintaining a focus on prevention of HIV disease. This Web site provides All About CAPS (program descriptions and CAPS research projects, a bibliography of CAPS publications, fact sheets and news, CAPS personnel) and lists positions available at CAPS. It also provides links to other AIDS/HIV Internet sites.

 Safer Sex Page

http://www.safersex.org/

This site has fact sheets, newsletters, brochures, forums, counseling information, and multimedia exhibits.

 ABBS

abbs-request@tde.com

"subscribe abbs"
　　Aids Bulletin Board Service

Owner: Norman Brown (norman.brown@tde.com)

 misc.health.aids

AIDS issues and support.

sci.med.aids

AIDS: treatment, pathology and biology of HIV, prevention (moderated).

 sci.med.immunology

Medical/scientific aspects of immune illness.

ALLERGIES

 Allergy Discussion List

listserv@tamvm1.tamu.edu

"subscribe allergy yourfirstname yourlastname"

 The Food Allergy Network

http://www.foodallergy.org/index.html

Patient-oriented site for answers to questions about common allergies.

 alt.med.allergy

Information and help for people with allergies.

ALZHEIMER'S DISEASE AND DEMENTIA

 Alzheimer's Association

http://www.alz.org/

This Web site provides information on the Women's Health Initiative Memory Study and other research and tests. It also identifies what's available at the association, chapter information, caregiver resources, medical information, advocacy activities, a reading list on Alzheimer topics. It also lists conferences and events and links to other Alzheimer-related materials on the WWW.

Alzheimer Web

http://werple.mira.net.au/~dhs/ad.html

Australian site that provides resources on books, articles, conferences, and research on Alzheimer's disease.

 Institute for Brain Aging and Dementia Homepage

http://maryanne.bio.uci.edu/

Comprehensive site for information about dementia.

 Alzheimer's Disease Research Center

majordomo@wubios.wustl.edu

"subscribe alzheimer"

Owner: Alzheimer's Disease Research Center, Washington University School of Medicine (alzheimer owner@wubios.wustl.edu)

 Candid-dementia

candid-dementia@mailbase.ac.uk

"join candid-dementia yourfirstname yourlastname"

AMPUTATION

 Amputee

listserv@sjuvm.stjohns.edu

"subscribe amputee yourfirstname yourlastname"

AMYOTROPHIC LATERAL SCLEROSIS

 Amyotrophic Lateral Sclerosis Association

http://www.alsa.org/tkomedia/alsa/

Information about the association and its publications.

 Amyotrophic Lateral Sclerosis Fact Sheet

http://www.caregiver.org/fs/fs_als.html

Produced by the Family Caregiver Alliance.

 Beat A.L.S.

http://www.phoenix.net/~jacobson/beatals.html

Major site for resources on ALS or Lou Gehrig's disease including the ALS Digest.

 ALS Interest Group

bro@huey.met.fsu.edu

Request to be added to the list.

Owner: Bob Broedel (bro@huey.met.fsu.edu)

 sci.med.diseases.als

ALS research and care.

ANXIETY AND PANIC ATTACKS

 alt.support.anxiety-panic

Support and discussion for people dealing with anxiety and panic attacks.

ARTHRITIS

 Arthritis Foundation

http://www.arthritis.org/

The Web site can help you learn more about arthritis and the work of the Arthritis Foundation. It allows you to search, connect to other arthritis organizations/foundations and other resources. It solicits contributions and membership, including benefits and publications. The American Juvenile Arthritis Organization (AJAO) and Arthritis and Rheumatism International (ARI) pages are on the Arthritis Foundation Web site.

 Arthritis Today

http://www.arthritis.org/at/

Magazine for people with arthritis.

 Arthritis Wise: Tips for Living Well with Arthritis

http://www.hsc.missouri.edu/arthritis/handtips.html

Information about joint protection, especially the hands.

 Rheumatoid Arthritis

http://www.duq.edu/PT/RA/PreventionOfDisability.html

Discusses the approaches used to reduce and prevent disability from becoming worse for people with RA.

 alt.support.arthritis

Support for persons with arthritis.

 misc.health.arthritis

Discussion of arthritis and related topics.

ARTHROPLASTY

 Health Links: Your Health

http://www.hslib.washington.edu/your_health/index.html

See sections on arthritis of the hip and of the knee.

ASTHMA

 alt.support.asthma

Discussion and support for people dealing with asthma.

ATAXIA

 alt.support.ataxia

Support for people with ataxia.

ATTENTION DEFICIT DISORDER

 Attention Deficit Disorder Archive

http://www.seas.upenn.edu/~mengwong/add/

Archival site for frequently asked questions from mailing lists on ADD.

 Children and Adults with Attention Deficit Disorder (CH.A.D.D.)

http://www.chadd.org/

Web page for the organization including information about the organization, descriptions of problems, legal and medical informations, tips for parents, and types of treatment.

DoctorNET Online Attention Deficit Links

http://www.comedserv.com/add.htm

Information about adult deficit disorder.

 Add-parents

majordomo@mv.mv.com

"subscribe add-parents"

 alt.support.attn-deficit

Primary subject is discussion of Ritalin and other medications.

AUTISM/ASPERGER'S SYNDROME

 Autism Resources

http://web.syr.edu/~jmwobus/autism/

One of the major resources on autism on the Internet. General resource on autism including publications, first person accounts, audiovisuals, libraries, and literature for sale.

 Dave's Autism Info Page

http://www.lancs.ac.uk/people/cpadak/autism/autism.htm

Provides information in England and is a mirror site for the Autism Resources page.

O.A.S.I.S. On-line Asperger's Syndrome Information and Support

http://www.udel.edu/bkirby/asperger

Special interest is research on high functioning autism and Asperger's Syndrome.

 On-The-Same-Page

http://amug.org/~a203/

Provides information on research, treatment, and news with links to numerous other sites.

 Autism and developmental disabilities

bit.listserv.autism

BLINDNESS

 American Council of the Blind

http://www.acb.org/

Provides information on the ACB activities and information.

 Blind Links

http://seidata.com/~marriage/rblind.html

Site is maintained by Ron Marriage and has a large selection of resources for persons with visual impairments.

 BlindFam

listserv@sjuvm.stjohns.edu

"subscribe blindfam yourfirstname yourlastname"

Blindnws

listxer@vml.nadak.edu

"subscribe blindnws yourfirstname yourlastname"

 Rplist (retinal pigmentosa and other degenerations)

listserv@stjohns.edu

"subscribe rplist yourfirstname yourlastname"

 alt.comp.blind-users

Newsgroup for persons who are blind.

 bit.listserv.blindnws

Discussion of issues related to blindness.

BURNS

 Shriners Home Page

http://pagemaker.com/~shriners/hospital.html

CANCER

 American Cancer Society (ACS)

http://www.cancer.org/

The ACS Web site contains information about ACS, programs and events, cancer information, meetings, extramural grants, publications, contributing, employment opportunities, and links to other (major) resources. It includes links to the Relay for Life, Breast Cancer Network, Great American SmokeOut, and Man to Man prostate cancer information.

CancerGuide

http://asa.ugl.lib.umich.edu/chdocs/cancer/CANCERGUIDE.HTML

CancerGuide is an electronic magazine on all aspects of cancer of interest to health professionals and patients.

CANSEARCH: A Guide to Cancer Resources

http://www.access.digex.net/~mkragen/cansearch.html

The National Coalition of Cancer Survivorship (NCCS) Cansearch Web site has hundreds of links to information on various kinds of cancer. It includes basic research, clinical trials, support, dealing with pain, help through the grieving process, general cancer publications, and information on various specific types of cancer. It also has information on NCCS and Cansearch.

OncoLink: Disease Oriented Menus

http://oncolink.upenn.edu/disease/

The OncoLink menus provide a list of cancer locations and links to those resources, which include various types of pediatric and adult cancers.

Breast-cancer

listserv@morgan.ucs.mun.ca

"subscribe breast-cancer yourfirstname yourlastname"

CancerNet

cancernet@cicb.nci.nigh.gov

"subscribe"

 Ovarian-Cancer

listserv@ist01.ferris.edu

"subscribe ovarian-cancer"

 alt.support.cancer

Support and information for people dealing with cancer.

 sci.med.diseases.cancer

Diagnosis, treatment, and prevention of cancer.

CARPAL TUNNEL SYNDROME

 Carpal Tunnel Syndrome

http://www.netaxs.com/~iris/cts/

Site provides a description of carpal tunnel syndrome and suggestions for prevention.

 Nerve Compression Syndromes

http://www.ohsu.edu/cliniweb/C10/C10.722.html#C10.772.491

Provides useful limits to sites discussing carpal tunnel syndrome and other nerve compression syndromes.

CEREBRAL PALSY

 United Cerebral Palsy Associations (UCPA)

http://www.ucpa.org/

The UCPS has hundreds of links to REACH OUT AND TOUCH: Technology Projects Group Initiatives, Assistive Technology Funding and Systems Change Project WWW site, UCPAs Techtots Project WWW site, UCPAs National Meetingplace Project (NMPP), disability-support connections, UCPAs employment services, UCPAs ADA OnLine Resource Center, and special events. It also provides information on The Cerebral Palsy (UCP) Research Foundation and UCP affiliate network.

 C-palsy

listserv@listserv.net

"sub c-palsy yourfirstname yourlastname"

 alt.support.cerebral-palsy

Cerebral palsy support and information.

CEREBROVASCULAR DISORDERS

 National Stroke Association

http://www.stroke.org/

Information about the organization's activities, publications, and resources.

 NINDS Stroke Information Guide

http://156.40.137.201/healinfo/disorder/stroke/strokehp.htm

National Institutes of Neurological Disorders and Stroke site on stroke.

Post-stroke rehabilitation

http://text.nlm.nih.gov/

Agency for Health Care Policy Research guidelines for poststroke rehabilitation. Select from a list of guidelines.

CHARCOT-MARIE-TOOTH DISEASE

 Charcot-Marie-Tooth Disease Information Exchange (CMT Net)

http://www.ultranet.com/~smith/CMTnet.html

Site provides information about the disease and a wide variety of sources that track the progress of education and research activities.

CHRONIC FATIGUE SYNDROME

 Cathar-M (magazine)

listserv@sjuvm.stjohns.edu

"sub cathar-m yourfirstname yourlastname"

 CFS-L Discussion Group

listserv@list.nih.gov

"sub cfs-l yourfirstname yourlastname"

 CFS-NEWS (newsletter)

listserv@list.nih.gov

"sub cfs-news yourfirstname yourlastname"

 CFS-WIRE

listserv@sjuvm.stjohns.edu

"sub dfs-wire yourfirstname yourlastname"

alt.health.cfids-action

Chronic fatigue syndrome action group (moderated).

 alt.med.cfs

Chronic fatigue syndrome discussion group (moderated).

 bit.listserv.cfs.newsletter

Chronic fatigue syndrome newsletter.

CYSTIC FIBROSIS

 Cystic Fibrosis

http://www.ai.mit.edu/people/mernst/cf/

This is an archival site for information about cystic fibrosis, which also provides links to other useful sites on CF.

 Cystic Fibrosis

http://www.kumc.edu/instruction/medicine/genetics/support/cystic_f.html

Site is maintained by the Kansas University Medical Center, which provides basic medical information about CF.

 Cystic Fibrosis Foundation

http://www.cff.org/

The Foundation provides grants for funding research on CF.

 Cystic-l

listserv@yalevm.cis.yale.edu

"subscribe cystic-l yourfirstname yourlastname"

DEAFNESS

 Deaf World Web

http://deafworldweb.org/dww/

Provides information worldwide about deafness including organizations, professional education, technology available, references, and captioning services.

 Deafblnd

listserv@ukcc.uky.edu

"subscribe deafblnd yourfirstname yourlastname"

 bit.listserv.deaf-l

Discussion of issues for people with deafness.

DEAFNESS AND BLINDNESS

 Australian DeafBlind Council

http://home.internex.net.au/~dba

DEPRESSION

 Clinical Depression Screening Test

http://sandbox.xerox.com/pair/cw/testing.html

Online screening test for depression.

Depressive Disorders

http://avocado.pc.helsinki.fi/~janne/mood/mood.html

Site is from Finland. It provides information and resources on depression and related disorders.

 Dr. Ivan's Depression Central

http://www.psycom.net/depression.central.html

Site is a clearinghouse for information on all types of depressive disorders and their treatment.

 Pendulum Resources

http://www.pendulum.org

Provides resources on education, commercial sites, and miscellaneous resources related to depression.

 Depress

listserv@soundprint.brandywine.american.edu

"subscribe depress yourfirstname yourlastname"

 Walkers-in-Darkness

majordomo@world.std.com

"subscribe walkers-in-darkness"

 alt.support.depression

Support and information for people dealing with depression and mood disorders.

alt.support.depression.manic

Support and discussion for people with bipolar disorders.

 soc.support.depression.crisis

Support group for people in crisis.

 soc.support.depression.family

Support group for families of people with depression.

 soc.support.depression.manic

Support group for people with bipolar disorders.

 soc.support.depression.misc

A general support group for all types of depression.

 soc.support.depression.seasonal

Support group for people with seasonal affect disorder.

 soc.support.depression.treatment

Support group for discussing treatment of depression.

DEVELOPMENTAL DISABILITIES

 alt.support.dev-delays

Support for people dealing with all types of developmental disabilities.

bit.listserv.down-syn

Down's syndrome discussion group.

DIABETES

 AACE Guidelines for the Management of Diabetes Mellitus

http://www.aace.com/guidelines/diabetes_guide.html

Site provides full text of the guidelines developed by the American Association of Clinical Endocrinologists.

 American Diabetes Association

http://www.diabetes.org/

Site provides information about the organization and publications provided by the association.

 Diabetic List

listserv@lehigh.edu

"subscribe diabetic yourfirstname yourlastname"

 Diabetic List Digest

listserv@lehigh.edu

"set diabetic digest"

 alt.support.diabetes.kids

Support for children dealing with diabetes.

misc.health.diabetes

Discussion of diabetes management in daily life.

DISABILITY: GENERAL

 The Abilities Website

http://www.ability.org.uk/

Site tries to focus on the abilities, not the disabilities, of persons with disabilities.

 Ability Network

http://www.ability.ns.ca/

Magazine for persons with disabilities. Site also provides links to other resources for persons interested in starting a business.

 Americans with Disabilities Act (ADA) Document Center

http://janweb.icdi.wvu.edu/kinder/

 Center for Independent Living (CIL)

http://www.wenet.net/~cil/

Organization in California that pioneered efforts to encourage persons with disabilities to live independently and not in an institution.

 Disability Net

http://www.disabilitynet.co.uk/

A British site that organizes numerous resources of interest to persons with disabilities.

disABILITY Information and Resources

http://www.eskimo.com/~jlubin/disabled.html

Site is written and maintained by Jim Lubin, who is a respirator-dependent quadriplegic, and provides access to a wide variety of resources on the Internet.

 Disability Info Center

http://www.geocities.com/capitalhill/3721/

Site provides access to a variety of links through its Best Disability Links on the Web.

 Do-It at the University of Washington Disability-Related Resources

http://weber.u.washington.edu/~doit/

Large site at the University of Washington, Seattle, which lists information about the Do-It Project but also provides links to many other sites of interest to persons with disabilities.

 Disability-Specific Web Sites

http://www.disserv.stu.umn.edu/disability/

Site provides links to numerous diagnoses related to disabilities. It is maintained by the University of Minnesota.

 Solutions@disability.com

http://disability.com/

Site is maintained by Evan Kemp Associates and organizes the links into 22 categories under the heading, "Disability Resources on the Internet."

 ADA-Law

listserv@vm1.nodak.edu

"subscribe ada-law yourfirstname yourlastname"

Dadvocat (for dads of disabled children)

listserv@ukcc.uky.edu

"subscribe dadvocat yourfirstname yourlastname"

 DS-H-PI

listserv@nihlist.bitnet

"subscribe ds-h-pi yourfirstname yourlastname"
    Physical independence and handicapped issues in International Classification of Impairments, Disability, and Handicaps.

 Mobility

listserv@sjuvm.stjohns.edu

"subscribe mobility yourfirstname yourlastname"

 alt.education.disabled

Discussion of educational needs and issues of people with disabilities.

 bit.listserv.easi

Computer information for people with disabilities. Easi means equal access to software and information.

 bit.listserv.l-hcap

Discussion of issues for people with disabilities.

 misc.handicap

General discussion group for people with disabilities.

**DISSOCIATIVE IDENTITY DISORDERS/
MULTIPLE PERSONALITY DISORDERS**

 alt.support.dissociation

Support for people with dissociative identity disorders.

DOWN SYNDROME

 Association for Children With Down Syndrome (ACDS)

http://macroserve.com/acds/acdshome.htm

The ACDS Web site includes a list of the members of the Executive Board, a letter from the Executive Director, ACDS publications list, and links to other Down syndrome WWW sites.

 Down Syndrome WWW Pages

http://www.nas.com/downsyn/

The Down Syndrome WWW page has been complied from the contributions of members of the Down Syndrome Listserv and identifies how to access Listserv. It also provides Information on Down syndrome, including articles, essays, organizations worldwide, toy catalogs, and other Internet resources for Down syndrome.

 National Association for Down Syndrome (NADS)

http://www.nads.org/

NADS provides a great bibliography of current books and videotapes on parent support, education issues, medical concerns, and adult issues. It also contains a list and links to Internet resources, as well as contact information on several support groups around the Chicago area.

National Down Syndrome Society (NDSS)

http://www.ndss.org/

The NDSS Web site includes general, clinical, and educational information, as well as information on research, advocacy, and affiliate and special programs. There are also links to Down syndrome pages on the Internet.

 Down-syn

listserv@vm1.nodak.edu

"subscribe down-syn yourfirstname yourlastname"

 Downs-research

downs-research@mailbase.ac.uk

"join downs-research yourfirstname yourlastname"

DYSPHAGIA

 Disease Processes and Dysphagia

http://www.dysphagia.com/diseases.htm

Discusses diseases that often have dysphagia as a problem.

 Dysphagia

majordomo@cyberport.com

"subscribe dysphagia"

DYSTONIA

 alt.support.dystonia

Support for people with dystonia.

EATING DISORDERS

 Alliance to Fight Eating Disorders (AFED)

http://www.fsci.umn.edu/~AAABL/

A volunteer organization in Minnesota devoted to public education about eating disorders.

 Anorexia Nervosa and Bulimia Association

http://qlink.queensu.ca/~4map/anabhome.htm

Canadian site with a quarterly newsletter that provides advice for living with eating disorders.

 Overeaters Recovery Group

http://www.hiwaay.net/recovery

Provides access to resources for people who are compulsive eaters.

 alt.support.eating-disord

Support for people with eating disorders.

EPILEPSY

 Comprehensive Epilepsy Management Center

http://balrog.aecom.yu.edu/epilepsy/index.html

Site is maintained jointly by Albert Einstein College of Medicine and the Montefiore Medical Center to provide information about epilepsy.

 alt.support.epilepsy

Support group for persons with epilepsy and their families.

FIBROSITIS AND FIBROMYALGIA

 Fibromyalgia Resources

http://www.hsc.missouri.edu/fibro/fibrotp.html

Provides answers to frequently asked questions about fibromyalgia.

 USA Fibromyalgia Association

http://www.w2.com/fibro1.html

Describes the organization and gives short descriptions of fibromyalgia and fibrositis.

 Fibrom-l

listserv@listserv.net

"sub fibrom-l yourfirstname yourlastname"

 alt.med.fibromyalgia

Support and discussion for people dealing with fibromyalgia or fibrosis.

FLUENCY—STUTTERING

 STUT-HLP

stut-hlp@bgu.edu OR stut-hlp@ecnuxa.bitnet

STUTT-L

stutt-L@templevm.bitnet

 STUTT-X

stutt-x@asuvm.inre.asu.edu OR Stutt-x@asuacad.bitnet

listserv@asuvm.inre.asu.edu

"subscribe stutt-x yourfirstname yourlastname"

FRAGILE X

 Fragile X

majordomo@counterpoint.com

"Subscribe fragilex youremailaddress"

GERIATRICS

 Aging Research Center

http://www.hookup.net/mall/aging/agesit59.html

Site for researchers in the field of aging. Information is fairly technical.

 Center on Aging

http://garnet.berkeley.edu/~aging

Berkeley, California site with information on careers in gerontology and the latest research on aging.

National Aging Information Center

http://www.ageinfo.org/

Site is designed to provide seniors with access to a variety of resources that may be useful, including information on public programs and policies.

 ### Geriatric-Neuropsychiatry

listserv@sjuvm.stjohns.edu

"subscribe geriatric-neuropsychiatry yourfirstname yourlastname"

 ### Gerinet

listserv@listserv.net

"sub gerinet yourfirstname yourlastname"

GRIEF/LOSS

 ### GriefNet

subscribe@rivendell.org

"subscribe griefnet youremailaddress"

GUILLAIN-BARRÉ SYNDROME

 ## Guillain-Barré Syndrome

http://www.adsnet.com/jsteinhi/html/accept/gbsagree.html

Jeff Steinhilber is a survivor of GBS who provides insight into the disorder and provides suggestions for coping with the problems.

Guillain-Barré Syndrome Fact Sheet

http://www.156.40.137.201/healinfo/disorder/guillain/guillain.htm

Site provides answers to frequently asked questions about Guillain-Barré.

 Guillain-Barré Syndrome Foundation International

http://www.adsnet.com/jsteinhi/html/gbs/gbsfi.html

Provides information about the organization and its activities.

HEADACHES

 alt.support.headaches.migraine

Support for people with migraines or other headaches.

HEAD INJURIES

 Acquired Brain Injury Forum

http://aztec.asu.edu/abi/welcome.html

Site is maintained by Perspectives network to provide information on support groups and resources for persons with brain injuries.

 The TBI Connection

http://www.seanet.com/~bobg/index.html

This Web page is dedicated to survivors of traumatic brain injury, their families, and organizations that have helped.

TPN Searchable Support Groups Database

http://www.sasquatch.com/cgi-bin/searchpage

Provides a "yellow pages" index to resources and services for persons and families dealing with traumatic brain injury.

 ### bit.listserv.tbi-support

Discussion and support group for people with head injuries.

HEARING IMPAIRMENT

 ### Hearing Loss Resources

http://www.webcom.com/houtx/welcome.html

Site is headquarters for the SayWhatClub providing information on hearing loss problems.

 ### Hereditary Hearing Impairment Resource Registry

http://www.boystown.org/hhirr/

Site is maintained by the Boys Town National Research Hospital to provide information and resources about hereditary conditions that may cause hearing loss.

 ### ASL-L

asl-l@connectamerica.com

 ### Audiol

audiol-l@bgu-edu

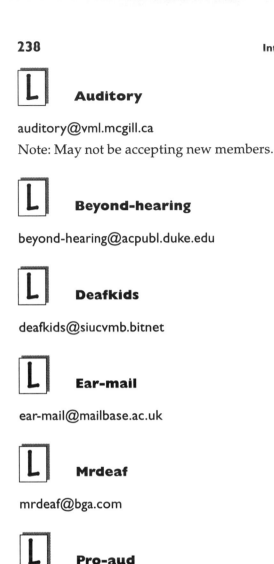

L   **Auditory**

auditory@vml.mcgill.ca

Note: May not be accepting new members.

L   **Beyond-hearing**

beyond-hearing@acpubl.duke.edu

L   **Deafkids**

deafkids@siucvmb.bitnet

L   **Ear-mail**

ear-mail@mailbase.ac.uk

L   **Mrdeaf**

mrdeaf@bga.com

L   **Pro-aud**

pro-aud@vml.cc.uakron.edu

L   **Slling-l**

slling-l@yalevm.ycc.yale.edu

HEART DISEASE

 American College of Cardiology

http://www.acc.org/

Site provides information on clinical publication, education programs, products, and use of computers in cardiology.

 American Heart Association

http://www.amhrt.org/

Provides information about the AHA, publications, and information about heart diseases.

Hemophilia

 alt.support.hemophilia

Support for people and families with hemophilia.

HUNTINGTON'S DISEASE

 Caring for People with Huntington's Disease

http://www.kumc.edu/hospital/huntingtons/

 Huntington's Disease—Research Highlights

http://www.156.40.137.201/healinfo/disorder/huntingt/hdreport.htm

Reports of the National Institutes for Neurologic Diseases on Huntington's.

Support Groups and International HD Organizations

http://www.kumc.edu/hospital/huntingtons/groups.html

Kansas University Medical Center maintains a major site on Huntington's disease.

HYDROCEPHALUS

 Hydrocephalus Association Home Page

http://neurosurgery.mgh.harvard.edu/ha/

Provides information about hydrocephalus and its treatment.

LEARNING DISABILITIES

 Dyslexia Archive

http://www.hensa.ac.uk/dyslexia.html

Archival site with numerous links to online resources.

 Dyslexia 2000 Network

http://www.futurenet.co.uk/charity/ado/index.html

Site for adults with long-standing dyslexia to find advice for addressing the problem.

 Landmark College

http://www.landmarkcollege.org/

Landmark College is an accredited college for persons with learning disabilities. The homepage provides many useful links to information about learning disabilities.

alt.support.learning-disab

Discussion group for individual with learning disabilities.

LUPUS

 Lupus Home Page

http://www.hamline.edu:80/~lupus/

Information on lupus for therapists and patients from the Lupus Foundation of America.

LYME DISEASE

 American Lyme Disease Foundation

http://www.w2.com/docs2/d5/lyme.html

Provides information on etiology and environmental management of Lyme Disease, including general precautions and recommendations.

 Lyme Disease Network

http://www.lehigh.edu/

Information from the Usenet group that includes guidelines for diagnosis and treatment, images of ticks, a newsletter, and general information.

 Lymenet-l

listserv@lehigh.edu

"subscribe lymenet-l"

sci.med.disease.lyme

Provides information about Lyme Disease, patient support, and research information.

MARFAN SYNDROME

 National Marfan Foundation

http://www.marfan.org/

webmaster@marfan.org

staff@marfan.org

Marfan syndrome is a potentially fatal genetic disorder of the connective tissue. This Web site provides information on conferences, publications/newsletters, support and contacts, connective issues, online resources, and people in the community.

 alt.support.marfan

Marfan syndrome support group.

MENTAL ILLNESS

 Internet Mental Health

http://www.mentalhealth.com/p1.html

Major resource on information about mental disorders.

 National Alliance for the Mentally Ill (NAMI)

http://www.nami.org/

Organization for people with mental illness with local affiliates throughout the United States.

Madness

listserv@sjuvm.stjohns.edu

"subscribe madness yourfirstname yourlastname"

 Outcmten (Assessing Outcomes)

listserv@sjuvm.stjohns.edu

"subscribe outcmten yourfirstname yourlastname"

 Traumatic-stress

mailbase@mailbase.ac.uk

"join traumatic-stress yourfirstname yourlastname"

 sci.psychology.psychotherapy

Discussion of psychotherapy.

MENTAL RETARDATION

 American Association on Mental Retardation

http://www.aamr.org/

Professional organization for persons working with persons with mental retardation.

 Association for Retarded Citizens (ARC)

http://thearc.org/

Organization for children and adults with mental retardation, which offers information and links to other resources.

MULTIPLE SCLEROSIS (MS)

 MS Direct Multiple Sclerosis Support

http://www.aguila.com/dean.sporlender/ms_home/

The MS Direct Web site is a tool to help find information and support locations on the internet. It contains news, links, a guestbook, disability resources on the Internet, and miscellaneous items.

 Multiple Sclerosis Foundation, Inc.

http://www.icanect.net/msf/

Provides information about programs and services.

 The Myelin Project

http://www.myelin.org/

The Myelin Project aims to accelerate research on myelin repair. This site contains a general orientation, research reports, and provides further information on publications, project events, how to reach us, and how you can help, as well as links to related organizations and sites.

 National Multiple Sclerosis Society

http://www.nmss.org/

The National MS Society Web site provides MS Information, local resources, identifies how you can get involved, and tells you about NMSS. It also provides links to other resources.

 Mslist-l

listserv@listserv.net

"sub mslist-l yourfirstname yourlastname"

alt.support.mult-sclerosis

Discussion group for multiple sclerosis.

MUSCULAR DYSTROPHY

 Families of Spinal Muscular Atrophy

http://www.abacus96.com/fsma

This SMA Web site contains information of interest to a person affected by SMA, family and friends of a person with SMA, or who works with those diagnosed with SMA. It has open letters to parents of newly diagnosed children, living with SMA, information and resources, and links to other SMA-related sites. It also states "How We Can Help You" and "How You Can Help Us."

For membership contact: sma@interaccess.com

 Muscular Dystrophy Association of Australia

http://www.mda.org.au/

This MDA site has received the "Cool Site—Top 1%" of the WEB Award and "Top 50 Site" Award by *Web Magazine* and is dedicated to Ryan Struck by his father Boris M. Struck, Executive Director, MDA. It has hundreds of links to resources on MD, a term that covers over 40 separate neuromuscular disorders, including spinal muscular atrophy (SMA).

Contact: Boris M. Struck, Webmaster bms@webnet.com.au

OBSESSIVE-COMPULSIVE DISORDER

 Obsessive-Compulsive Disorder Resource Center

http://www.suncompsvc.com/ocd/index.html

Provides definition, resources available, and suggests for patients and relatives for coping with the disorder.

OCD-L

listserv@vm.marist.edu

"subscribe ocd-l yourfirstname yourlastname"

 alt.support.ocd

Support for people with OCD

OSTEOGENESIS IMPERFECTA

 alt.support.osteogenesis.imperfecta

Discussion and support for people with osteogenesis imperfecta.

OSTEOPOROSIS

 National Osteoporosis Foundation

http://www.nof.org/

Describes osteoporosis, provides information on treatment and prevention, guidelines for care, risk factors, bone health, and political activities to increase awareness of osteoporosis.

 sci.med.diseases.osteoporosis

Osteoporosis information exchange.

PARALYSIS AND SPINAL CORD INJURIES

 American Paralysis Association

http://maryanne.bio.uci.edu/apa/

Organization for education about spinal cord injuries, which includes teaching aids and graphics.

 Cure Paralysis Now!

http://www.cureparalysis.org/

Dedicated to research on paralysis, this site includes a wide range of materials on spinal cord injuries.

 Hub

http://www.inch.com/~dog666/hub/

Lists many individuals' homepages who have disabilities as well as links to many other sites for persons who use wheelchairs.

 Spinal Cord Injury Support Network

http://www.brainlink.com/~phil/

Major resources for information on spinal cord injuries.

PARKINSON'S DISEASE

 James Parkinson Organization

http://james.parkinsons.org.uk/index.htm

This Web site is concerned with all aspects of living with Parkinson's Disease.

Parkinsn

listserv@vm.utcc.utoronto.ca

"subscribe parkinsn yourfirstname yourlastname"

 Parkinson's Disease Information Center

http://gladstone.uoregon.edu/~jskaye/pd/

Provides information, statistics, and resources about Parkinson's disease.

 Parkinson's Web

http://neuro-chief-e.mgh.harvard.edu/parkinsonsweb/Main/PDmain.html

Major resource on Parkinson's disease maintained by Harvard University, which includes information on support services, research updates, bibliographies, and other Internet resources.

PEDIATRIC DISORDERS

 PEDINFO Congenital Disorders

http://www.uab.edu/pedinfo/DiseasesCongenital.html

Covers many of the major congenital disorders in children.

 PEDINFO Index

http://www.uab.edu/pedinfo/index.html

Provides useful links to other pediatric Web pages.

POLIO AND POST-POLIO SYNDROME

 Polio Survivors Page

http://www.eskimo.com/~dempt/polio.html

A clearinghouse for information about polio and post-polio syndrome.

Polio

listserv@sjuvm.stjohns.edu

"sub polio yourfirstname yourlastname"

 alt.support.post-polio

Post-polio syndrome discussion group.

REPETITIVE STRAIN INJURY

 RSI-UK

listserv@tictac.demon.co.uk

"subscribe rsi-uk yourfirstname yourlastname"

 misc.health.injuries.rsi

Provides expert answers to questions about RSI (moderated).

RETT SYNDROME

 International Rett Syndrome Association

http://www2.paltech.com/irsa/irsa.htm

Provides information about Dr. Rett's observations, medical research, publications, and membership applications.

ROTATOR CUFF

 Rehabilitation after surgery

http://weber.u.washington.edu/~dboone/key/subjects/arthritis/zrwtwrzzl_l.html

Patient education information given after rotator cuff surgery.

SCHIZOPHRENIA

 Schiz-l

listproc@list.ab.umd.edu
"subscribe schiz-l yourfirstname yourlastname"

 Schizoph

listserv@vm.utcc.utoronto.ca
"subscribe schizoph yourfirstname yourlastname"

 alt.support.schizophrenia

Patient and family support group for schizophrenia.

SENSORY INTEGRATIVE DYSFUNCTION

 Sensory Integration

http://www.autism.org/si.html
Page by Cindy Hatch-Rasmussen, M.A., OTR/L

 Sensory Integration

http://www.nmark.com/si/
Page by Marie E. DiMatties and Norma J. Quirk.

SEXUAL ABUSE SURVIVORS

 Recovery

recovery@wvnvm.wvnet.edu
Send message asking to join.
Moderator: Jeff Brooks (jeff@wvnvm.wvnet.edu)

SJÖGREN'S SYNDROME

 Sjögren's Syndrome Foundation

http://www.sjogrens.com/

Provides a clinical description, differential diagnosis, and symptoms.

SPINAL CORD INJURIES

 Scipin-l

listserv@albnydh2.bitnet

"subscribe scipin-l yourfirstname yourlastname"

STROKE

 Stroke-l

listserv@ukcc.uky.edu

"subscribe stroke-l yourfirstname yourlastname"

STUTTERING

 Stuttering

listproc2@bgu.edu

"subscribe stut-hlp yourfirstname yourlastname"

SUICIDE

 SAVE-Suicide Awareness, Voices of Education

http://www.save.org/

Site provides lists of warning signs of potential suicide, especially depression, so that prevention can be started before suicide is attempted.

 Suicide FAQ

http://www.lib.ox.ac.uk/internet/news/faq/archive/suicide.info.html

Archival site dedicated to discussion of suicide. Site provides answers to the frequently asked questions about suicide, its treatment, and recovery of families experiencing suicide.

THORACIC OUTLET SYNDROME

 Nerve Compression Syndromes

http://www.ohsu.edu/cliniweb/C10/C10.772.html#C10.722.491

Provides information and links to other resources on thoracic outlet syndrome.

 Thoracic Outlet Syndrome

http://www.156.40.137.201/healinfo/disorder/thoracic/thoracic.htm

Site is maintained by the National Institutes of Health to provide basic information about the syndrome.

TOURETTE'S SYNDROME

 Tourette's Syndrome Information Site

http://www.ccn.cs.dal.ca/Health/Tourette/TS.html

Site is sponsored by the Tourette's Syndrome Foundation of Canada to provide information and resources for persons interested in Tourette's syndrome.

 Tourette's Syndrome Home Page

http://www.personnel.umd.umich.edu/~infinit/tourette.html

Information about myths and realities of Tourette's syndrome including associated disorders.

TUBERCULOSIS

 Tuberculosis Resources

http://www.cpmc.columbia.edu/tbcpp/

Provides description and graphics of tuberculosis useful for patient education.

TUMORS

 BRAINTMR

listserv@mitvma.mit.edu

"Subscribe braintmr"provides information on brain tumors.

Owner: Samantha Scolamiero samajane@sasquatch.com

VESTIBULAR DISORDERS

 Vestibular Disorders Association (VEDA)

http://www.teleport.com/~veda/

Site provides patient-oriented information about vestibular disorders such as Meniere's, labyrinthitis, and endolymphatic hydrops.

VIOLENCE

 National Center for Injury Prevention & Control: Division of Violence Prevention

http://www.city-net.com/~/mann/women/resources/index.html

Provides facts and bibliographies about violence.

 Victorian Institute of Forensic Medicine

http://worldmall.com/erf/lectures/env-23.txt

Series of lectures about violence.

WOMEN'S HEALTH

 Women's Health Hotline

http://www.soft-design.com/softinfo/womens-health.html

Full text of their newsletter.

 Women's Health Hot Line Home Page

http://www.catalog.com/softinfo/womens-health.html

Tracks information about women's health in the media.

Women's Health Weekly

http://www.homepage.holowww.com/1w.htm

Online weekly newsletter with abstracts of research projects on issues in women's health.

 Women's Medical Health Page

http://www.best.com/~sirlou/wmhp.html

 Wh-news

listserv@uwavm.u.washington.edu

"subscribe wh-news yourfirstname yourlastname"

JOB OPPORTUNITIES

 Medsearch

http://www.medsearch.com/

 Tomorrow's OT, Tomorrow's PT, Tomorrow's SLP

http://www.targetmarket.com/

REHABILITATION FACILITIES

 Center for Psychiatric Rehabilitation

http://web.bu.edu/SARPSYCH/

Courage Center

http://freenet.msp.mn.us/ip/health/courage_center/top.html

 Craig Hospital

http://www.csn.net/rehab/

 Department of Rehabilitation Medicine at the University of Colorado Health Sciences Center, Denver, Colorado

http://www-uchsc.edu/sm/sm/deptremd.htm

 Florida Hospital Rehabilitation Services

http://www.flhosp.org/rehab/

 Florida Sunshine Rehabilitation

http://www.senior.com/fsr/whois.html

 Glenrose Rehabilitation Hospital

http://www.grhosp.ab.ca/rehab.htm

 Harmarville Rehabilitation Center

http://www.harmarville.org/

 Magee Rehabilitation, Philadelphia, Pennsylvania

http://www.mageerehab.org/

NMSS: Rehabilitation

http://www.nmss.org/cmsi/cmsi153.html

 Northeast Rehabilitation Hospital—RehabNET

http://www.rehabnet.com/

 Rehabilitation Learning Center, Harborview Medical Hospital, Seattle, Washington

http://weber.u.washington.edu/~ric/

 Rehabilitation & Research Center, Virginia Commonwealth University

http://griffin.vcu.edu/html/pmr/rrc/pmrrrc.html

 Rusk Institute of Rehabilitation Medicine, New York, New York

http://www.med.nyu.edu/Rusk/rusk.html

 University of Chicago

http://www.uic.edu/depts/mcpm/cog_rehab.html
http://www.uic.edu/depts/mcpm/inpt_rehab.html

Hand Rehabilitation/Hand Therapy

 Hand Rehabilitation Program—Parkland Health and Hospital System

http://www.swmed.edu/home_pages/parkland/par/hand.html

Hand Rehabilitation Center

http://www.lumc.edu/lumc/patcar/specisrv/sshandre.htm

 Michigan Hand Rehabilitation Center

http://www.michhand.com/

Neurodevelopmental Therapy (NDT)

 NDT Information

http://www.iceseminars.com/index.htm

PUBLISHERS OF REHABILITATION BOOKS

 Lippincott-Raven Publishers: Physical Therapy/Occupational Therapy

http://www.lrpub.com/allied.htm

This Web site contains information on books by author, books by title, journals, and newsletters that are published by Lippincott-Raven. Ordering information is also given for ordering online, by telephone, by fax, and by mail.

 Majors' Medical Books

http://www.majors.com/booklist.html

The J.A. Majors' Home Page Web site is the largest distributor of health science (including occupational therapy) books and multimedia titles in the United States.

 Mosby/Time Inc.

http://www.mosby.com/Mosby/Catalogs/AlliedHealth

National Institutes for Mental Health

http://www.nimh.nih.gov/nimh.web

 Slack Inc. OT/PT Resources

http://www.slackinc.com/otpt/otpt.htm

http://www.slackinc.com/wwwslack.htm

Slack is a major publisher of occupational and physical therapy resources.

 Williams & Wilkins Publishers

http://www.wwilkins.com/books/

DATA BASES AND DOCUMENT DELIVERY

 Carl Uncover

http://www.carl.org/

A document delivery service for articles published in the past few years. Searching the tables of contents of the journals is free but copies of the articles range from $6 to $18 per article depending on how the copy of the article (document) is to be sent. Articles can be sent priority (2-day delivery), overnight, or fax. Requester must provide a credit card number to order.

 MEDLINE Database

http://www.healthgate.com/

Provides free searching on the last 2 years of the MEDLINE data base.

U.S. National Library of Medicine

http://www.nlm.nih.gov/

Provides access to the data bases maintained by the National Library of Medicine. Most require an access code except the National Library of Medicine catalog.

CLINICAL SCIENCES

 ATLAS Advanced Tools for Learning Anatomical Structure

http://www.med.umich.edu/lrc/Atlas/atlas.html

Offers three courses in anatomy including gross anatomy, embryology, and histology.

 Brain Anatomy Image

http://www.med.harvard.edu/BWHRad/BrainSPECT/BrSPECT.html

Provides anatomic images of the brain.

 Gateway to Neurology

http://132.183.145.103/

Site is maintained by the Massachusetts General Hospital and provides online chapters on neurologic disorders.

 Muscles in Action

http://www.med.umich.edu/lrc/Hypermuscle/

Site provides information on muscle actions and movement.

Neuroanatomy Study Slides

http://www.mcl.tulane.edu/student/1997/kenb/neuroanatomy/readme_neuro.html

Excellent series of slides on neuroanatomy with text to explain each slide. Slides can be displayed with or without identifying information for self-study and examination.

 Neuroscience

http://www.neuro.fsu.edu/

Site in maintained by Florida State University and includes a comprehensive list of resources on many aspects of neuroscience.

 Psychiatry

http://www.psych.med.umich.edu/web/psychref/disorder

Site is a data base of information on psychiatric disorders and treatment.

 Visible Human Project

http://www.nlm.nih.gov/research/visible/visible_human.html

Provides anatomic cross-section views of the human body.

CLINICAL SUBJECTS

Biomechanics and Movement Science

 biomch-l

listserv@sic.sufnet.nl

"subscribe biomch-l yourfirstname yourlastname"

Growth and Development

 Cogdevel

listserv@unccvm.bitnet

"subscribe cogdevel yourfirstname yourlastname"

 Motordev

listserv@umdd.bitnet

"subscribe motordev yourfirstname yourlastname"

Neurology and Neuropsychology

 Brain-l

listserv@mcgill1.bitnet

"subscribe brain-l yourfirstname yourlastname"

 Child-neuro

child-neuro@waisman.wisc.edu

Ask to be put on mailing list.

 **Child-neuro-parent**

child-neuro-parent@wiasman.wisc.edu

Ask to be put on mailing list.

 **Neurl**

listserv@uicvm.bitnet

"subscribe neurl yourfirstname yourlastname"

 **Neuro**

listserv@emgmhs.mcg.edu

"subscribe neuro yourfirstname yourlastname"

 **Neurol-l**

listserv@uicvm.uic.edu

"subscribe neurol-l yourfirstname yourlastname"

 **Neuromc**

neuromotor-request@ai.mit.edu

Ask to be put on mailing list.

Neuropsyc

mailbase@mailbase.ac.uk

"join neuropsyc yourfirstname yourlastname"

Orthopedics

 Ortho-l

listserv@gait2.gait.ohio-state.edu

"subscribe ortho-l yourfirstname yourlastname"

Physical Medicine and Rehabilitation

 Rehab-ru

listserv@ukcc.uky.edu

"subscribe rehab-ru yourfirstname yourlastname"

Prevention and Wellness

 Longevity

listserv@vm3090.ege.edu.tr

"subscribe longevity yourfirstname yourlastname"

 Maxlife

listserv@gibbs.oit.unc.edu

"subscribe maxlife yourfirstname yourlastname"

 Wellnesslist

majordomo@wellnessmart.com

"subscribe wellnesslist yourfirstname yourlastname"

Psychiatry

 ### Child-psychiatry

mailbase@mailbase.ac.uk

"join child-psychiatry yourfirstname yourlastname"

Sports Medicine

 ### AMSSMNet

listserv@msu.edu

"subscribe AMSSMNet yourfirstname yourlastname"
  American Society for Sports Medicine

 ### Atntrn-l

listserv@iubvm.ucs.indiana.edu

"subscribe athtrn-l yourfirstname yourlastname"

 ### Sports psychology

listserv@vm.temple.edu

"subscribe sportpsy yourfirstname yourlastname"

 ### Sportscience

list@stonebow.otago.ac.nz

"subscribe sportscience yourfirstname yourlastname"

THERAPIES

Behavioral Analysis

 Behav-an

listserv@vml.nadak.edu

"subscribe behav-an yourfirstname yourlastname"

Cognitive Rehabilitation

 SCR-L

Listserv@mizzoul.missouri.edu

"subscribe scr-l yourfirstname yourlastname"

Functional Electrical Stimulation

 Fes-l

listserv@ualtavm.bitnet

"subscribe fes-l yourfirstname yourlastname"

Hypnosis

 Hypnosis

listserv@netcom.com

"subscribe hypnosis"

Orthotics and Prosthetics

 Oandp-l

listserv@nervm.nerdc.ufl.edu

"subscribe oandp-l yourfirstname yourlastname"

APPENDIX A

■ ■

Internet Quiz

1. **Which of the following statements about the Internet is true?**
   a. The Internet was started during World War II.
   b. The Internet is worldwide.
   c. The Internet is available only to the government and research universities.
   d. The Internet is used primarily for business transactions.

2. **Which of the following is required to access the Internet?**
   a. A login code
   b. A password
   c. A personal identification number
   d. None of these

3. **Which of the following Internet services provides real-time interaction with other users?**
   a. Chat
   b. E-mail
   c. Usenet
   d. Bulletin board

4. **Which of the following products lets you browse the World Wide Web?**
   a. Bunyip
   b. Eudora
   c. Trumpet
   d. Netscape

5. Which of the following is the central authority of the Internet?
   a. The Department of Defense
   b. The Advanced Research Projects Agency
   c. The National Science Foundation
   d. There is no central authority.

6. Which of the following is (are) the standard protocol(s) required for a computer to be connected to the Internet?
   a. FTP
   b. TCP/IP
   c. ISP
   d. POP

7. In the Internet address *jsmith@watson.bcm.edu* which is the highest level domain?
   a. jsmith
   b. watson
   c. bcm
   d. edu

8. Which of the following will a search engine be able to locate?
   a. Web documents
   b. Gopher menus
   c. FTP files
   d. All of the above

9. Which of the following allows you to subscribe to a discussion group?
   a. Usenet and mailing lists
   b. FTP and Gopher
   c. E-mail and World Wide Web
   d. BBS and Archie

10. Which of the following is used to create Web documents?
    a. ISDN
    b. HTML
    c. SLIP
    d. TCP/IP

11. Which of the following programs provides text-only access to the World Wide Web?
    a. Mosaic
    b. Eudora
    c. Cello
    d. Lynx

12. Which of the following Internet resources allows you to download software and files to your computer?
    a. Gopher
    b. FTP
    c. Archie
    d. E-mail

13. Which of the following Internet resources allows you to access a remote computer and functions as a terminal to that computer?
    a. Telnet
    b. Search engine
    c. Veronica and Jughead
    d. World Wide Web

14. Which symbol is used in an E-mail address to separate the username from the host computer name?
    a. *
    b. @
    c. ^
    d. #

15. Which of the following statements about the World Wide Web is true?
    a. It was developed at the beginning of the Internet.
    b. Graphics, sound, and text-based resources are linked on the Web.
    c. The browser must be a GUI-based browser.
    d. Subjects of interest must be selected from a menu of choices.

16. Which part of the URL http://www.library.tmc.edu/texsearch.html identifies the Internet address as a Web site?
    a. http://
    b. www.library.tmc.edu
    c. texsearch
    d. HTML

17. Which of the following Netscape menus or buttons allows you to access a previously visited Web site without re-entering the URL?
    a. File
    b. Open
    c. Reload
    d. Bookmark

18. **Which of the following is generally the first link to a Web site?**
    a. The home page
    b. The root directory
    c. The search form
    d. The Gopher server

19. **A hyperlink may point to:**
    a. A music file
    b. A text file
    c. A video file
    d. Any of the above

20. **To limit the number of "hits" in a search on** *space shuttle* **which of the following logical operators would you use?**
    a. And
    b. Or
    c. Not
    d. But

21. **Which Internet resource was designed as a text-based resource that allows you to "tunnel" down through a series of menus to find Internet documents?**
    a. E-mail
    b. FTP
    c. Gopher
    d. Archie

22. **Which file transfer mode is appropriate for transferring graphic files?**
    a. ASCII
    b. Binary
    c. Text
    d. Font

23. **Which is the login ID at most FTP sites from which anyone may download files?**
    a. FTP
    b. Anonymous
    c. Hello
    d. Dear Sir

24. **Which of the following resources will Archie locate?**
    a. Gopher sites
    b. FTP files and directories
    c. HTTP resources
    d. Web pages

25. **A group of people discussing the same subject in the same area of IRC is called a:**
    a. Newsgroup
    b. Chat room
    c. Forum
    d. Talkie

ANSWERS

1. b	6. b	11. d	16. a	21. c
2. d	7. d	12. b	17. b	22. b
3. a	8. d	13. a	18. a	23. b
4. d	9. a	14. b	19. d	24. b
5. d	10. b	15. b	20. a	25. b

Adapted from Brauer, R. T., & Marx, G. (1996). *Exploring the Internet.* Upper Saddle River, NJ: Prentice Hall.

APPENDIX B

■■■■■■■■■■■■■■■■■■■■■■■■■■■■■■

Modem Lights and What They Mean

AA   Auto Answer. The modem is set up to answer the telephone.

ARQ   Automatic Repeat Request. When lit, error correction is functioning.

CD   Carrier Detection. Modem is connected to another modem.

CTS   Clear to Send. The CTS output from the modem is operational.

DTR   Data Terminal Ready. The modem is ready to send or receive.

EC   Error Correction. When lit, error-correction protocols are functioning.

FAX   Modem is connected to a fax machine.

HS   High Speed. Modem is ready to communicate at its highest speed.

LAP   Modem is using LAPM error correction.

MNP   Modem is using MNP 1–4 error correction.

OH   Off Hook. Lights when modem picks up telephone to dial.

RD   Receive Data. Modem has received bytes from another modem.

RTS   Ready to Send. The modem is ready to work.

SD   Send Data. Modem is sending data. Same as TD.

SYN   Synchronous Mode. Modem is transmitting synchronously.

TD   Transmit Data. Modem is transmitting data. Same as SD.

TE   Transmission Error. Indicates an LAPM or MNP transmission error.

TR   Data Terminal Ready. The modem is ready to send or receive.

APPENDIX C

■ ■■■■■■■■■■■■■■■■■■■■■■■■■■■■■■■■■ ■

Internet Sources

The following list is representative of references available about the Internet but is not comprehensive.

Books

(1996). *Your personal net doctor: Your guide to health and medical advice on the Internet and online services.* New York: Wolff New Media. Reviews more than 2,000 health sites. Updates are provided at the Web site www.ypn.com. Written for consumers.

Cedeno, N. (1995). *The Internet tool kit.* San Francisco: Sybex. Guide to useful tools on the Internet, where to find them, and how to use them.

Cheong, F. C. (1996). *Internet agents: Spiders, wanderers, brokers, and bots.* Indianapolis, IN: New Riders Publishing. For advanced Internet users. Information about agent programs including search engines.

Cotton, B., & Oliver, R. (1994). *The cyberspace lexicon: An illustrated dictionary of terms from multimedia to virtual reality.* London: Phaidon Press Limited. A good illustrated dictionary.

Crumlish, D. (1995). *The Internet dictionary.* San Francisco: Sybex. Provides definitions for more than 2,400 terms.

December, J., & Randall, N. (1996). *World Wide Web unleashed 1996.* Indianapolis, IN: Sams.net. Comprehensive guide to the Web.

Eager, B. (1994). *Information superhighway illustrated.* Indianapolis, IN: Que. Good graphics and illustrations of how the Internet works, with brief descriptions.

Eager, W., Donahue, L., Forsyth, D., Mitton, K., & Waterhouse, M. (1995). *Net.Search.* Indianapolis, IN: Que. Good reference for locating information on the Internet.

Ferguson, T. (1996). *Health online.* Reading, MA: Addison-Wesley. Contains sources on medical Internet sites.

Gibbons, D., Fox, D., Westernbroek, A., Cravens, D., & Shafran, A. B. (1994). *Using E-mail: The complete reference to electronic mail*. Indianapolis, IN: Que. Good text on use of E-mail.

Gibbs, S. R., Sullivan-Fowler, M., & Rowe, N. W. (1996). *Mosby's Medical Surfari*. St. Louis: Mosby. Rates top health care Internet resources for content, response rate, resource type, and special requirements (eg, extra software).

Gilster, P. (1996). *Finding it on the Internet: The essential guide* (2nd ed.). New York: Wiley. Good explanation of the major Internet clients and browsers.

Gilster, P. (1996). *The new Internet navigator*. New York: Wiley. Fairly thorough reference for dial-up access to the Internet.

Gralla, P. (1996). *How the Internet works: All new edition*. Emeryville, CA: Ziff-Davis Press. Provides excellent visual display of how the Internet works and describes the various resources.

Hahn, H. (1996). *The Internet: Complete reference* (2nd ed.). Berkeley, CA: Osborne McGraw-Hill. Good thorough reference to the Internet.

Hogarth, M., & Hutchinson, D. (1996). *An Internet guide for the health professional* (2nd ed.). San Diego: Authors. Written by a physician and a nurse. Lists sites to most medical specialties and nursing sites.

Honeycutt, J. (1995). *Using the Internet with Windows 95: The fast and easy way to learn*. Indianapolis, IN: Que. Contains the disk Internet Explorer 2.0. and easy to follow instructions for using Windows 95 to access the Internet.

Jamsa, K., & Cope K. (1995). *World Wide Web directory*. Las Vegas, NV: Jamsa Press. Shows pictures of Web pages and includes CD-ROM.

James, P. (1996). *Official Netscape Navigator 2.0 Book*. Research Triangle Park, NC: Ventana Communications Group. Provides useful information and explanation of how to use Netscape to access different aspects of the Internet.

Kientzle. T. (1995). *Internet file formats*. Scottsdale, AZ: The Doriolis Group. Good resource for multimedia files and includes a CD-ROM.

Kraynak, J., Fulton, J., Kinkoph, S., & Weiss, A. (1996). *The big basics book of the Internet*. Indianapolis, IN: Que. Good basic instructions with illustrations.

LeBlanc, D. A., & LeBlanc. R. (1995). *Using Eudora: The user-friendly reference*. Indianapolis, IN: Que. Useful reference on this E-mail program.

Levine, J. R., & Baroudi, C. (1995). *Internet secrets*. Foster City, CA: IDG Books Worldwide. Discusses more advanced topics about the Internet.

Levine, J. R., & Baroudi, C. (1996). *Internet for dummies* (3rd ed.). Foster City, CA: IDG Books. Popular introduction to the Internet.

Linden, T., & Kienholz, M. L. (1995). *Dr. Tom Linden's guide to online medicine*. New York: McGraw-Hill. Lots of useful health and medicine sites. Some sites do not have an updated Web page address including Ron Stone's site at the University of Puget Sound.

Madison, E. (1995). *How to use America Online* (2nd ed.). Emeryville, CA: Que. Illustrated instructions on using America Online.

Meyers, S., & Pinch, C. (1996). *The downloader's companion for Windows* (2nd ed.). Englewood Cliffs, NJ: Prentice Hall. Contains program files for many helper applications.

Oliver, D. (1996). *Netscape 2*. Indianapolis, IN: Sams.net Publishing. Comprehensive reference on Netscape and includes a CD-ROM.

Pfaffenberger, B. (1996). *Web search strategies*. New York: MIS Press. Details information about using search tools to locate information on the Internet.

Rosch, W. L. (1995). *Multimedia Bible*. Indianapolis, IN: Sams Publishing. Good reference on multimedia and includes a CD-ROM.

Rositano, D. J., Rositano, R. A., & Stafford, R. D. (1996). *Que's mega Web directory*. Indianapolis, IN: Que. List over 18,000 Web sites and includes a CD-ROM with hotlinks to every site listed.

Rowland, R., & Kinnaman, D. (1995). *Researching on the Internet*. Rocklin, CA: Prima Publishing. Very good resource on how to use the Internet successfully.

Ryer, J. C. (1995). *A pocket tour of health & fitness on the Internet*. San Francisco: Sybex. Many sources of good sites on the Internet.

Sattler, M. (1995). *Internet TV with CU-SeeMe*. Indianapolis, IN: Sams.net. Discusses using CU-SeeMe, a videoconferencing software program.

Schwerin, R. (1996). *How to use Netscape Navigator 2.0*. Emeryville, CA: Ziff-Davis Press. Illustrated instructions on Netscape.

Setter, C. (1995). *The Internet for Macs for dummies*. Foster City, CA: IDG Books. Popular introduction to using Macs to access the Internet.

Young, M. L., & Levine, J. R. (1995). *Internet FAQs*. Foster City, CA: IDG Books Worldwide. Excellent resource. Answers many questions about the Internet.

Young, M. L., & Levine, J. R. (1996). *Internet for Windows for dummies starter kit*. Foster City, CA: IDG Books. Popular introduction to using Windows to access the Internet.

Journals and Newsletters

Boardwatch Magazine, 8500 W. Bowles Ave., Suite 210, Littleton, CO 80123. http://www.board-watch.com

I-way, P.O. Box 538, Peterborough, NH 03458-9950. http://www.cciwcb.com/

Internet 20. Subscriptions, Emap Readerlink, Audit House, Field End Road, Eastcote, Ruislip, Middlesex HA4 9LT, England http://www.emap.com/Internet/

Internet & Java Advisor, P.O. Box 469048, Escondido, CA 92046-9753. http://www.advisor.com/

Internet Medicine, Lippincott-Raven Publishers, P.O. Box 1600, Hagerstown, MD 21741-9910.http://www.lrpub.com/

Internet World, P.O. Box 7461, Red Oak, IA 51591-2461. http://www.iworld.com/

Internet Underground, 1920 Highland Ave., Suite 222, Lombard, IL 60148. http://www.underground-online.com/

Java Report, Sigs Publications, Inc., P.O. Box 5049, Brentwood, TN 37024-9737. http://www.signs.com/

Medicine on the Net, COR Healthcare Resources, P.O. Box 40959, Santa Barbara, CA 93140-0959. cor-info@corhealth.com

Microsoft Interactive Developer, Fawcette Technical Publication, 209 Hamilton Ave., Palo Alto, CA 94301-2500. 75451.2343@compuserve.com

Multimedia Online, 660 Bleachland Blvd., Suite 300, Vero Beach, Fl 32963. getmmo@aol.com

.net, P.O. Box 301070, Escondido, CA 92030-9942. http://www.futurenet.co.uk/net.html

NetGuide, P.O. Box 420355, Palm Coast, FL 32142-9371. http://www.netguide.com/

Online Access, Subscription Department, 5615 W. Cermak Road, Chicago, IL 60650-9884. http://www.redflash.com/

The Net, P.O. Box 56136, Boulder, CO 80323-6136. http://www.thenet-usa.com/

VirtualCity, P.O. Box 3007, Livingston, NJ 07039-9922. http://www.vcwn.com/

Visual Developer, 7339 E. Acoma Dr. # 7, Scottsdale, AZ 85250-9748. http://www.coriolis.com/

Web Bound, N.A. International, 2001 Mentor Rd., Louisville, TN 37777. http://www.webbound.com/

WEB Developer, P.O. Box 7463, Red Oak, IA 51591-2463. http://www.developer.com/

Web Techniques, P.O. Box 58730, Boulder, CO 80323-8730. http://www.webtechniques.com/

Websight. Customer Service, P.O. Box 2441, Cupertino, CA 95015-9957. http://websight.com/

Websmith, P.O. Box 55549, Seattle, WA 98155. http://www.ssc.com/websmith/

Webweek, P.O. Box 3072, Northbrook, IL 60065-3072. http://www.iword.com/

Wired, P.O. 191427, San Francisco, CA 94119-9708. No Internet address given.

Yahoo! Internet Life, P.O. Box 53381, Boulder, CO 80323-3381. http://www.yil.com/

Glossary of Terms

Analog: Information expressed in a continuous display of a physical quality, for example, sound waves, mercury in a thermometer, and a sweep watch with hands.

Anonymous FTP: Internet file transfer protocol resource allowing a user to connect to a site, search through file directories, and download a file, document, or program.

Application: A computer program belonging to a class of software designed to provide instructions to manage and perform a specific computing task.

Archie: An Internet computer program client and service designed to locate files from public FTP sites and provide the address and path to the specific file(s) designated in the search. Archie is the oldest of the Internet browsers.

ARPANET: (Advanced Research Projects Agency Network). This precursor of today's Internet started in 1969 to connect the University of California and Stanford Research Institute. It was retired in 1990.

ASCII: (American Standard Code for Information Interchange). ASCII character set allows different computer types to share information using the standard 138 ASCII characters described in a 7-bit code.

ATM: (Asynchronous transfer mode). An international standard for cell relay. Multiple service types (voice, data, video) are conveyed in small, fixed-size cells.

Bandwidth: A term for specifying the amount of information a cable or other medium can handle simultaneously. Greater bandwidth is needed to handle increased volume on Internet traffic and transfer video and audio files.

Baud: A term used to measure the speed of a modem connection.

Binary code: The use of 0s and 1s in a string of bits is called binary code. Code strings of 7 bits in length are called ASCII character set; code strings in 8 bits are called extended character set. All information stored in a computer is in binary code. Term also describes computer program files that are not text (ASCII) files.

Bits: The lowest unit of information on a computer, a binary digit. A bit can have the value of 0 or 1.

Bits per second. (bps): A measure of the number of bits transferred per second over a communication channel such as a modem. The higher the number of bps, the faster the modem.

Bookmark: A link created on a Web browser to connect directly to a site without having to type the site name or number in the Open or Location box of the browser.

Boolean operator: Used to define search criteria when searching data bases such as WAIS or MEDLINE. Common Boolean operators are AND, OR, NOT.

bps: See bits per second. A measurement of data transmission speed.

Bridge: A computer server that connects two local area networks that use the same protocol language. Used on LANs that have grown so large that performance is degraded.

Browser: A computer program client used to search Gopher or the World Wide Web. Refers to the ease of use of these programs.

Bulletin board service. (BBS): A computer using communication software that is set up to allow callers to connect to it using a modem. It provides electronic space for the posting and exchange of messages and files.

Byte: A group of bits that represent one letter or number in the computer's memory. A byte contains 8 bits. An example is 00110101. There are 256 possible combinations. Many documents and programs are measured in bytes. For example, an average page of text has 250 words or 1,000 to 2,000 bytes.

Cache: A reserved memory space on a computer for storing frequently required instructions. They can be sent quickly because they are either in the form of dedicated circuitry (hardware cache) or in the dynamic RAM memory (software cache).

CD-ROM. (Compact disk read-only memory): One CD can hold 650 megabytes of information or about 400,000 pages of text, which is the reason an entire encyclopedia can be placed on one CD-ROM.

Central processing unit. (CPU): The computer's microprocessor that can be thought of as the computer's brain or chief executive office.

CGI. (Common gateway interface): An application program interface (API) used on Unix operating machines that allows a Web server to pass data from an hypertext markup language document to a CGI script.

Channel: Virtual area where Internet relay chat (IRC) users communicate in real time.

Chat: A service provided on many bulletin boards and online services that permits two-way exchange of messages as they are typed in real time, as opposed to E-mail, which incurs a lag between the sending and receiving of a message.

CIX: Commercial Internet Exchange. A nonprofit trade association of public data Internet service providers. It promotes and encourages development of the public data communication internetworking services.

Client: A computer program that makes a request for services to another computer, called a server. Each client program provides access to a specific type of server although some clients are multipurpose and therefore can work with several types of servers.

Clock speed: The speed (in megahertz) at which the CPU or microprocessor is able to process information.

Command line: An interface or computer program that requires text commands to activate programs or features such as DOS requires. Compare to graphic user interface.

Communications software: Any software application program that facilitates the exchange of information with another computer.

COM port: Serial port on IBM PC compatible computers, usually used for data communications and referred to as COM1, COM2, COM3, or COM4.

Compression protocol: In data transmission, a set of rules for reducing the size of a file so it can be transmitted in less time or stored in less space.

Configuration: The method of setting up hardware or software to perform selected functions. For example, a modem can be set up (configured) to send information at 2,400, 9,600, or 14,400 bits per second.

Connect time: The period of time during which a user is signed onto the system such as an online service, bulletin board system, host computer, or Internet service provider.

CPS. (Characters per second): Characters refer to a single 8-bit byte of data.

CPU: See central processing unit.

CSU/DSU. (Customer service unit/digital service unit): A hardware device that provides a digital interface to high-speed leased lines. It looks and acts like a modem, but it does not modulate or demodulate the signal from digital to analog because it deals with digital signals only.

Daemon: A Unix program that runs in the backgroup but is available to perform a specific task when needed. It may provide a message saying an E-mail is undeliverable or to alert the user when new E-mail messages have been received.

Data base: A program that stores data on a designated topic. MEDLINE and library catalogs are examples of data bases.

DNS. (Domain name server): A two-column table system of matching mnemonic names to the numeric Internet protocol address.

Domain name: The unique addresses of a computer on the Internet, comprised of several subdomains that are used to group computers together (.ac [academic], .co [commercial]).

Domain name server: The computer on which the domain name and the names of users are kept.

Dot pitch: A measure of the proximity of the holes through which beams of light project an image on a computer display. A smaller dot pitch produces a sharper image.

Download: The process of getting files from a remote host computer to a local computer over a communication link.

Driver: In computing, a small file of instructions needed to make an operating system such as Windows aware of the hardware such as a video card, printer, modem, or CD-ROM drive.

Dumb terminal: A terminal that does not contain an internal central processing unit.

Duplex: A terminal emulation setting choice when configuring communication software. A full duplex link permits data to be sent and received simultaneously; half duplex must alternate between sending and receiving data.

Electronic mail. (E-mail): Messages delivered using an electronic network to an electronic mailbox where they can be read, replied to, and saved.

Emulation: Using one type of computer to mimic or act like the operation of another. For example, the Macintosh can run special software so that it acts as though it were a PC running Windows.

Encryption: A process of coding information so it cannot be read or used without proper authority. One use of encryption on the Internet is scrambling a credit card number so someone cannot copy the number for unauthorized use.

Error correction protocol: In data transmission, a set of rules used by modems to ensure that a transmitted file is received intact with no parts missing.

FAQ: See frequently asked questions.

FDDI. (Fiber distributed data interface): An ANSI standard defining a 100-Mbps token-passing network using fiberoptic cable. Transmission distance can be over a mile without repeaters.

Fiberoptics: A method of transmitting light beams using optical fibers.

File compression: Special software is used that makes the files smaller allowing them to be transmitted more rapidly and taking less room on the hard drive.

File suffix: An acronym attached to the filename that indicates the type of file or program necessary to expand or decode it. Usually the acronym is three letters such as .zip. Also called file extension.

File transfer protocol. (FTP): Part of the TCP/IP protocol suite of computer files used on the Internet for transferring files across TCP/IP connections. Usually files that can be FTPed are held in public archives at FTP sites. Using an FTP client the files can be retrieved.

Firewall: A security gateway designed to protect the internal network of computer from unauthorized access.

FIX. (Federal Internet Exchange): A network exchange point that interconnects federal government networks together and to the Internet.

Flame: A hurtful, harmful, or derogatory computer message typed in response to another message. A "flame war" results when the hurtful messages continue to go back and forth between two or more people.

Flow control: See handshaking.

Freeware software: The author of the computer program owns the copyright but has made the program available free of charge.

Frequently asked questions. (FAQ): A text file of questions and answers commonly asked by new users of listservs, Usenets, Gophers, and so forth or a record of information about a topic that is available for perusal. (Repeating the same information becomes boring for the more experienced user.)

FTP: See file transfer protocol.

Gateway: A computer that serves as a communication link between two different kinds of networks using different operating systems. The gateway computer converts information into a compatible format before passing it along the other network.

Gigabyte. (GB): One billion bytes. Used to describe the size of large hard drives and data bases.

Gopher: An Internet service that organizes information on the Internet into a series of hierarchical menus. Also the name of the client (computer program) that accesses Gopher sites.

Graphic user interface. (GUI): The use of visual features such as point and click, icons, drag and drop, pulldown menus, and windows to facilitate computing tasks. Contrast to command-line interface in which commands must be typed from memory or a list.

GUI: See graphic user interface.

Handshaking: A method of regulating the flow of data between two modems and between the modem and computer. Handshaking ensures that the device will not be sent too much information at once. Also called flow control.

Helper application: A short computer program needed by a client such as a Web browser to provide access to functions not contained with the client, such as the ability to play a sound file or act as a Telnet client.

Home page: The default hypertext page to be loaded by the Web browser client when it first appears on the screen.

Host computer: Refers to the computer on a network that provides services to many users. In relation to the Internet the host computer is the one that runs the service software with which users interact by means of a client program.

HTML: See hypertext markup language.

HTTP: See hypertext transfer protocol.

Hyperlink: An emphasized word, phrase, or image that when selected (clicked) leads to another document.

Hypertext: A document or page containing links to other documents or pages. The user can move from one document to another by clicking on any marked link.

Hypertext document: A document or Web page with computer-activated links embedded in the text or graphic to connect to other documents.

Hypertext markup language. (HTML): A format used by the Web to create hypertext documents.

Hypertext transfer protocol. (HTTP): The set of rules used by Web sites to maintain hypertext links.

Icon: A picture used to represent a computer program, file, or function.

Initialization: In communication, the first set of instructions used to instruct the modem to send and receive data. They are based on a set of commands developed by Hayes, an early manufacturer of modems.

Integrated services digital network. (ISDN): High-speed digital telephone lines that send data transmission rates at 64,000 bps or higher by sending the data as a stream of bits, instead of first converting the data to analog or sound using a modem.

Interface: The way the computer is set up for the user. The two most typical are command line and graphical user.

Internet: A worldwide network of networked computers using the TCP/IP protocol suite. Informally the ability to exchange E-mail with other Internet users.

Internet protocol (IP) address: A unique identifying number assigned to every computer directly connected to the Internet. The address is composed of four groups of numbers separated by dots. Most people prefer to use the easier letters to remember the domain name.

Internet service provider. (ISP): Companies or individuals who lease time and access to lines that are connected to the Internet through a host computer or router. Prices vary depending on the type of service available and amount of connect time the user wants.

Internet services: A general term for applications available over the Internet. Basic tools are electronic mail, file transfer protocol, and Telnet. Newer tools including Archie, Gopher, wide area information server, and the World Wide Web are based on the basic application.

InterNIC. (Internet Network Information Center): A major source of information about the Internet and directory services that also registers domain names. AT&T Corporation coordinates the information and directory services; Network Solutions Inc. coordinates the domain name registration.

IRC. (Internet relay chat): A type of interactive communication on the Internet, which occurs in real time.

ISDN: See integrated services digital network.

ISP: See Internet service provider.

JAVA: A software language used to create documents on the Internet. To view JAVA documents the computer must be using a program that can read 32 bits such as Windows 95.

JPEG. (Joint Photographic Experts Groups): A standard for digital photographic images.

Jughead: A search client used to search or scan the Gopher site directories on which Jughead resides. See Veronica.

Kbps. (Kilobits per second): A measure of data transmission speed.

Kilobyte. (KB): One thousand bytes.

LAN. (Local area network): A group of computers located in a specific area and connected to a server, which allows them to communicate with each other.

Laser printer: A printer that uses a laser to dry the ink distributed on the page. Laser printers are faster and provide sharper images than dot matrix or ink jet printers. Laser printers are recommended for printing documents from the Internet.

Leased line: An expensive high-speed constant connection to the Internet that is leased from an Internet service provider or telephone company.

Link: A word or graphic used to link the current document of a hypertext document to another.

Listserv: A type of mailing list used to manage a discussion group.

Local area network. (LAN): A network of computers physically located at the same site or within a relatively small geographic area.

Login or Logon: Entering a user personal number and password or personal identification number (PIN) to sign on to a site. Public passwords are anonymous or guest.

Mail server: A program used to manage E-mail. Some mail servers are used primarily to manage mailing lists such as Listserv, whereas others are used to send files from FTP archives by E-mail such as FTP mail. Mail servers are used by Internet service providers to manage E-mail for dial-up users.

Mailing list: A list of names and addresses of people who will all receive the same copy of a message sent to the mailing list. Lists are organized by topics, subjects, or specialties.

Megabyte. (MB): One million bytes.

Memory: The amount of information that can be stored or used on a computer.

MIME: See multipurpose Internet mail extensions.

Modem: A device designed to facilitate communication among computers using telephone lines. The sending modem converts digital information into analog sound for transmission (**mo**dulation), while the receiving modem reconverts the signal back to digital (**dem**odulation)

Modulation protocol: The protocol used by both modems in a communication link that governs the basic speed of the signal. The protocols include V.22bits, V.32, V32bis, and V.34.

Monitor: The visual display screen, housing, and controls used to adjust the characteristics of the screen image.

Mouse: In computers, a mechanical device used to operate the computer along with the keyboard. The mouse is represented on the screen as a cursor.

MPEG. (Motion Picture Experts Groups): A standard for compressing digital video images.

Multimedia: Computer-based application that provides information or entertainment in the user in the form of several types of media including sound, text, graphics, video, photographs, or animation.

Multipurpose Internet mail extensions. (MIME): A standard for the ASCII encoding of binary files, such as movie or graphics, so they can be sent by E-mail on the Internet.

NAP. (Network access point): One of the four primary connections to the Internet designed by the National Science Foundation to provide connections to regional network providers.

Netiquette: A code of acceptable behavior, Internet etiquette, expected of all users.

Network: Linking several computers and their peripherals, such as printers, together to enable resources to be shared and to facilitate communication between the users of those computers.

Network news transfer protocol. (NNTP): The protocol used on the Internet to exchange Usenet news.

Newsgroup: A bulletin board type of discussion group that uses the Usenet protocol. Each group has "threads" of discussion about different topics going on at the same time. Messages remain for a few weeks and then are removed. Some may be archived. Usenet groups are arranged in a hierarchical system with names grouped around nine topics.

News server: A computer running NNTP software that permits a news reader client to retrieve items from Usenet groups.

Offline reader: A software program client that can automatically gather E-mail and other messages from an online service and then disconnect from the service. The user reads the collected messages after the client has disconnected, in other words, offline. Replies are stored by the client until the next time the client is connected online and can send the replies online.

OLE. (Object linking and embedding): Capability introduced with Windows e.1 that gives Windows application a standard for incorporating objects created in other Windows programs.

Online: In the context of telecommunication, the act of connecting (going online) or being connected to an online service, bulletin board, or other network service.

Online service: A large commercial network offering online access plus many additional resources and services to a large number of people who pay a monthly service fee.

Packet switching: A message delivery protocol in which information is divided into small units (packets) and then relayed through routers on the computer network.

PCMCIA. (Personal Computer Memory Card International Association): A slot in a laptop into which an external device the size of a credit card can be inserted. PCMCIAs can be modems, hard drives, or video devices.

Ping: An application program that indicates if a particular host computer is presently connected to the Internet.

Pixel: Derived from the term *picture element*, the individual dots of light that make up the image on the screen of a monitor.

Point of presence. (POP): A bank of modems supplied by an Internet service provider, often permitting access to their high-speed TCP/IP network by way of a local call.

Point-to-point protocol. (PPP): A network interface that allows dial-up users to temporarily connect their computers to the Internet and use TCP/IP-based clients. It is generally preferred to the alternative serial line Internet protocol.

Port: A connection on the back of a computer to which an external device can be connected or a setting within the computer.

Post office protocol. (POP3): A protocol used on the Internet for storing and retrieving E-mail.

Protocol: A type of computer program that enables interactions between computers on the Internet such as hypertext transfer protocol. It contains a system of rules and procedures governing communications between two devices.

Public domain: A category of software in which the author does not chose to maintain copyright, permitting use of the program without getting the author's permission or making a payment.

Remote imaging protocol. (RIP): A type of terminal emulation using graphic elements stored on the caller's computer to rapidly draw color screens.

Router: A device such as a computer that connects two or more networks.

Search engines: A term applied to software programs that look for information in response to a query made by a user. A number of search engines have been developed for the Web to help locate files on the Internet.

Serial communications port: A hardware interface used to connect a device such as a modem or printer to the computer. Serial refers to the sending and receiving of data one bit at a time. Serial ports use handshaking.

Serial line Internet protocol. (SLIP): A network interface that allows dial-up users to temporarily connect their computer to the Internet and use TCP/IP-based clients. It is an older standard than the alternative, point-to-point protocol.

Server: A program that receives requests for information from a client program, locates the information, and sends it back to the client or user. A server directs the sharing of resources among many users on a multiuser host.

Shareware: A category of computer program software that users can try for a specified evaluation period before buying.

Shell account: Used on Unix machines to provide access to the Internet.

Simple mail transport protocol. (SMTP): The computer program protocol used on the Internet for sending and receiving E-mail

SLIP: See serial line Internet protocol.

SMTP: See simple mail transfer protocol.

Super video graphics array. (SVGA): A graphics standard for PCs requiring compliant systems to be capable of displaying a screen resolution of 800 × 600 or 1024 × 768 pixels. More than 256 colors at these resolutions may be supported.

System operator. (sysop): Some times called the administrator, a sysop is a person who runs, or is responsible for, a bulletin board or online service.

T1: A classification of telephone lines offering 23 voice channels and one supervisory channel or 1.544 Mbps digital data service.

TCP/IP: See transfer communication protocol/Internet protocol.

Telecommunications: Communications over telephone lines, whether a conversation between people or the exchange of digital information between computer or fax machine.

Telemedicine: The use of telecommunications technologies and computers by health care providers to overcome barriers in health care delivery such as physical distance and lack of locally trained personnel.

Telnet: The software program protocol that forms part of the TCP/IP protocol suite used on the Internet. Also an Internet service, where a Telnet client emulates a "virtual Internet terminal" allowing remote access to a host computer.

Terabyte. (TB): One trillion bytes.

Terminal emulation: The imitation (emulation) of a physical terminal by communication software. A terminal emulator can be used over a telecommunications link to interact with a host that might be many miles away. Popular terminal types to emulate include vt100, TTY, and ANSI.

Transmission control protocol/Internet protocol. (TCP/IP): A computer program protocol suite including transmission control protocol, Internet protocol, SMTP, FTP, Telnet, and many other protocols operating on the Internet.

Treading: Selecting and reading all messages in a particular conversation subject in the sequence in which they were posted, rather than reading all messages and all subjects.

Uniform resource locator. (URL): A standardized syntax used on the Internet describing the location and method of accessing Internet resources. Each URL is composed of several elements including the domain name of the host, the port address, and the pathname.

Unix: A computer-operating system designed to support multiple simultaneous users. Hosts running on Unix are predominant on the Internet.

Usenet: A type of conferencing system in which messages related to a particular subject are distributed to the newsgroup over the Internet and other networks. Usenet does not rely on TCP/IP-based networks for message distribution and therefore is not strictly an Internet service.

Uuencode: The name of computer program originating on Unix machines, now a standard for the ASCII encoding of binary files so they can be sent by E-mail on the Internet.

V.34: International standard for modem data communication at speeds up to 28,800 bps.

Veronica: The name of a search engine that locates files, documents, and directories indexed by Gopher.

Virtual reality: The computer generated simulation of a physical environment that permits interaction with the "virtual" objects within it.

Virus: A small segment of software code created to get into a hard disk, causing the computer to malfunction or lose data. Virus detection software can scan for unusual activity that might be caused by a virus.

WAN: See wide area network.

Wide area information server. (WAIS): A computer server that supports client access to a data base indexing the full contents of documents pertaining to a certain topic.

Wide area network. (WAN): A network of computers, not physically located in the same small geographic area. The arrangement is often used to connect two parts of an organization that are separated by some distance within a city.

Winsock: A Dynamic Link Library (DLL) program for Microsoft Windows.

World Wide Web (WWW): An Internet service that uses hypertext links to connect with other sites widely distributed over the Internet. Web pages may include graphics and other multimedia elements.

INDEX

■■

INSTRUCTIONS FOR USING INTERNET GUIDE FOR REHABILITATION PROFESSIONALS SOFTWARE

In an effort to help you use *Internet Guide for Rehabilitation Professionals* as efficiently as possible, we have provided the links from the book as a simple HTML file. Using the file on the enclosed floppy disk, you can easily locate all the sites and services mentioned in the book simply by clicking. This file will work with any web browser.

To use the enclosed disk on a Microsoft Windows system:

1. Follow the normal steps to run the web-browsing software you would like to use.
2. Insert the enclosed floppy disk into your disk drive.
3. Select "Open" or "Open File in Browser" from the File menu. (The exact name of this command may vary slightly depending on the browser you're using.)
4. Type **A:\rehab.htm**
5. Use the alphabetical menu at the top of the screen and the scrollbars to locate the entry or entries you are interested in. Click on the entry title to go to that resource. For E-mail and mailing list addresses, click on the address to compose and send mail. (If you are subscribing to a mailing list, carefully note the subscription instructions.)

To use the enclosed disk on a Macintosh system:

1. If you use Macintosh system version 7.0 or higher, you can mount and read the enclosed DOS-formatted disk just as you would a standard Macintosh-formatted disk.
2. Follow the normal steps to run the web-browsing software you would like to use.
3. Insert the enclosed floppy disk into your disk drive.
4. Select "Open" or "Open File in Browser" from the File menu. (The exact name of this command may vary slightly depending on the browser you're using.)
5. Click on the "Desktop" button.
6. Double-click on the icon for the floppy disk you inserted. (If you can't see it in the window immediately, use the scrollbar to locate it.)
7. Double-click on the file "rehab.htm."
8. Use the **Find** command or the vertical scrollbar to locate the entry or entries you are interested in. Click on the entry title to go to that resource. For E-mail and mailing list addresses, click on the address to compose and send mail. (If you are subscribing to a mailing list, carefully note the subscription instructions.)